Falling Into Love

THE TRANSFORMATIVE POWER OF COMMUNITY

LANG CHARTERS

BALBOA.PRESS
A DIVISION OF HAY HOUSE

Copyright © 2020 Lang Charters.

All rights reserved. No part of this book may be used or reproduced by any means, graphic, electronic, or mechanical, including photocopying, recording, taping or by any information storage retrieval system without the written permission of the author except in the case of brief quotations embodied in critical articles and reviews.

Scripture quotations marked MSG are taken from THE MESSAGE, copyright © 1993, 2002, 2018 by Eugene H. Peterson. Used by permission of NavPress. All rights reserved. Represented by Tyndale House Publishers, a Division of Tyndale House Ministries.

Scripture quotations taken from the New American Standard Bible® (NASB), Copyright © 1960, 1962, 1963, 1968, 1971, 1972, 1973, 1975, 1977, 1995 by The Lockman Foundation Used by permission. www.Lockman.org

Scripture quotations marked (NIV) are taken from the Holy Bible, New International Version®, NIV®. Copyright © 1973, 1978, 1984, 2011 by Biblica, Inc.™ Used by permission of Zondervan. All rights reserved worldwide. www.zondervan.com The "NIV" and "New International Version" are trademarks registered in the United States Patent and Trademark Office by Biblica, Inc.™

Scripture quotations are from New Revised Standard Version Bible, copyright © 1989 National Council of the Churches of Christ in the United States of America. Used by permission. All rights reserved worldwide.

Balboa Press books may be ordered through booksellers or by contacting:

Balboa Press
A Division of Hay House
1663 Liberty Drive
Bloomington, IN 47403
www.balboapress.com
1 (877) 407-4847

Because of the dynamic nature of the Internet, any web addresses or links contained in this book may have changed since publication and may no longer be valid. The views expressed in this work are solely those of the author and do not necessarily reflect the views of the publisher, and the publisher hereby disclaims any responsibility for them.

The author of this book does not dispense medical advice or prescribe the use of any technique as a form of treatment for physical, emotional, or medical problems without the advice of a physician, either directly or indirectly. The intent of the author is only to offer information of a general nature to help you in your quest for emotional and spiritual well-being. In the event you use any of the information in this book for yourself, which is your constitutional right, the author and the publisher assume no responsibility for your actions.

Any people depicted in stock imagery provided by Getty Images are models, and such images are being used for illustrative purposes only.
Certain stock imagery © Getty Images.

Cover Art: Melanie Peterson

Print information available on the last page.

ISBN: 978-1-9822-4940-3 (sc)
ISBN: 978-1-9822-4942-7 (hc)
ISBN: 978-1-9822-4941-0 (e)

Library of Congress Control Number: 2020910513

Balboa Press rev. date: 07/07/2020

I dedicate this book to friends and family everywhere. You make a huge difference, mean the world to me, and are loved more than words can say!

Contents

Acknowledgments ix
Preface to the Preface xi
Preface xiii

Chapter 1   A Day That Changed My Life 1
Chapter 2   Warheads and Princesses 5
Chapter 3   The Wink 13
Chapter 4   Dying and a Cry for Help 23
Chapter 5   I Made It to the Hospital, so Everything
            Should Be Okay ... Right? 31
Chapter 6   The Healing Power of Community 39
Chapter 7   You Are What You Think 51
Chapter 8   Laughing, Crying, and Everything in
            Between: Being Present to Ourselves and Others ... 63
Chapter 9   The Setback 79
Chapter 10 Vampire Love 93
Chapter 11 I Don't Know 101
Chapter 12 A Christmas to Remember 117

Epilogue 131
Pictures 133

Acknowledgments

I'm deeply grateful to Leia, Lee, Kathy, Rick, Kate, Lawrence, Matt, Erick, Kevin, Scott, Julie, and more because our conversations and your sharing about the accident and the months following it were instrumental in crafting this book. Thank you, Lisa, Kathy, and Sue, for reading and helping me edit it. Finally, without the support and encouragement of my wife, Lisa, this may never have happened. Thank you!

Preface to the Preface

This book is meant for everyone. How does one write a book with a strong Christian slant and emphasis while also keeping it friendly and inspiring to non-Christians? I'm not sure, but I'm going to try. I lead chapters with Bible verses and write quite a bit about God and Jesus, but if those words are problematic for you, I'd ask you to still give this book a chance. If it helps you to replace *God* with *Spirit, Source, Creator, the Mystery Behind Reality, the Divine, reality, love,* or something else, please do so. After all, words for the Divine are nothing more than metaphors and signposts for the Spirit, beautiful beyond words. Above all, my heartfelt desire is for my experiences and musings to encourage us to love and care for one another a little more ... and hopefully connect more with something bigger than and beyond ourselves!

Preface

> Let me give you a new command: Love one another. In the same way I loved you, you love one another. This is how everyone will recognize that you are my disciples—when they see the love you have for each other. (John 13:34–35, The Message)

When I was young my dad was in the army, so we traveled and moved quite a bit. Later, as an adult, I served as an officer in the air force, so again I visited a lot of places and lived in several. One constant in both of these times, and the rest of my life for that matter, was church. And by *church*, I don't mean a building, a Sunday service, or even only Christians. I mean people. To narrow the point further, a consistent and life-giving, life-saving blessing I've experienced has been to love, be close to, be connected with, and be loved by communities of beautiful people.

My assignments in the air force included San Antonio, Tucson, and Las Vegas, and each time I moved, I prayed over and over to get connected with a group of Christ followers. I asked God to meet people who were roughly my age and shared similar interests, with the intent of both hanging out together and spurring one another to grow closer to and more like Christ. Every time, my prayers were more than answered.

Ironically, when I moved, my primary motivation in asking God for new friends was communal fun and transformation. Little did I know we would end up doing life together, sharing the highs, lows, and everything in between. What started out as a "God, I especially like eating, drinking, playing board games, enjoying movies, watching sports, and playing computer games, so having people to do those things with would be fantastic" from my end turned into a group of friends who loved one another in tangible, life-giving, healing, and life-saving ways.

My longest air force assignment was at Davis-Monthan Air Force Base in Tucson, Arizona, and it was there I formed some of my closest and deepest friendships. In a matter of months, a weekly small-group Bible study transformed into a group of friends who also ate, laughed, and played together virtually every Friday night and often on the weekends. Over time, we became so close that we gave ourselves a name, the Crew. Amy, myself, Matt, Ali, Martha, Danny, Kevin, Andrea, and Matt (who I instantly knew would be my friend because his last name is Lang and my middle name is Matthew) eventually grew to include Erin, Ross, Tina, Sara, Mike, Sarah, Dave, and Susan.

For a good while, our time together was largely fun and games. But, as seems to happen when people enter their thirties, life started getting messy, so we also began sharing the burdens of journeying through the messiness together. We have loved each other during and through miscarriages, breakups, lost jobs, career changes, divorces (only mine, and hopefully it stays that way), parenting struggles, and cancer, among other things.

The self-sacrificial, others-oriented love of the Crew and other communities of friends has been a game changer in my life. These communities of love are, and have been, life-giving, life-changing, and life-saving. I'm convinced this Christlike love I experienced with my friends is the most powerful force in the universe.

God is love and loves every single person in the world. Because we're made in the image of God and are crafted to reflect our Creator to each other, most of our experience of God's love occurs in relationships with others. In short, God's love for us and toward us reveals itself while transforming and healing us in community. *Falling into Love* is a tale of communally surrendering to, resting in, being held by, and radiating this big love.

1

A Day That Changed My Life

> And we know that God causes all things to work together for good to those who love God, to those who are called according to His purposes. (Romans 8:28 New American Standard)

Red Rock Canyon, in the desert just outside Las Vegas, is a stark yet beautiful landscape. It features few plants or trees but is littered with vibrant, burgundy-colored rocks varying in size from pebbles to boulders and even plateaus. Jagged mountains, many of them in the distinctive dark red that the area is named for, curve around the park on three sides, forming a bowl of sorts so that almost every vantage point gives good views of the mountains. As I hiked the trails on November 10, 2008, with my fiancée, Kate; my three-year-old daughter, Lara; and Kate's son, eight-year-old Leif, we spied rock climbers scaling cliffs in the distance, a common sight in the park. It was the kind of day you dream about and remember fondly for the rest of your life.

Kate and Leif had come to visit Lara and me for a long weekend in Las Vegas, which was my current duty station as an officer in the air force. Kate was a successful and smart thirty-two-year-old. At the time, she had been in banking for about ten years, starting as a teller and working her way up to bank branch manager. Kate had captured my heart for numerous reasons. She had a smile that lit up her face—the kind that subconsciously makes a person think the room has just gotten brighter. Whenever I saw her grin, it made me want to do likewise. She had hazel eyes that were soft yet intense at the same time. Those eyes looked into mine and seemed to gaze into the depths of my soul. Kate's eyes combined with her mind to notice more than the average person. For instance, she asked, "Why is it at restaurants, a customer gets charged extra for adding something to her meal but does not get a discount for taking items out?"

Kate and I viewed the world in similar ways. We both wanted to help those less fortunate. We liked Mexican food, loved to eat dinner at a good sushi restaurant, enjoyed wine, laughed at the same parts in movies, and had become close friends. We lived in different states, but we talked on the phone for two or three hours every night, intimately getting to know each other. Kate's boy, Leif, was everything I could hope for in a stepson: smart, kindhearted, eager to learn, and very well behaved. He was the kind of boy who follows his requests with a respectful *please* and is sure to show his appreciation with a thank-you.

Because of our long-distance relationship, Kate and I saw each other only every few weeks, and we had spent time together with both of our kids on only a couple of occasions, which made this visit extra special. During the weekend, we laughed, kissed, held hands, played with the kids, ate at the Cheesecake Factory (who can turn down dinner followed by great cheesecake?), watched movies, and had an excellent time together.

Most picture Las Vegas as a pretty hot place, but on a fall day like November 10, the weather was practically perfect. The temperature was in the sixties, and the sky was sunny after raining the night before. So it was that following my usual morning run, Kate and I took the kids to Red Rock Canyon.

The park was covered with rocks, boulders, and larger formations painted magenta by nature. In places they were stacked one atop another, creating a series of rocky hills and valleys. Most of these formed fairly gentle inclines, and as we walked, we passed several other groups of hikers.

We strolled around the park while taking pictures and enjoying ourselves. "I like your yellow tank top," I told Kate.

Falling Into Love

Kate was the designated photographer, so at one point, the kids and I got a little ahead of her, and one of us—no one remembers which—spotted a cave that was a short hike away. We all took a look and readily agreed that we wanted to explore it. I set about searching for a good path to take to it while Kate and the kids stood back.

At the time, we were on a large, flat plateau that was big enough that although the kids stood near the center and could see the formation's edges, they couldn't see down to the ground some thirty feet below. At the edge of the plateau, and a step down from the main surface, lay a path leading to the cave. In other words, the hollow was around the corner to the left, at the end of the trail.

Kate and the kids stood in the middle of the formation on top while I went to the side to get on the trail below. I sat down and put my feet on the ledge. As I stood, my feet unexpectedly slipped out from under me, dropping me back on my butt, which pitched me forward. It was not a violent, vault-into-the-air movement but a completely-caught-off-guard type of spill with forward momentum that pitched me swiftly toward the edge of the ledge. I tried to plant my feet, but they kept sliding on the rocks that were a little slippery from the previous night's rain. I frantically attempted to grab the nearby rocks to halt my progress, but my hands could not find a good enough purchase. Skidding on the rock and loose dirt toward the edge of a cliff, I couldn't do anything to stop my momentum. I soared out into empty space.

I flew off the cliff and fell headfirst like I was diving into a lake—only there was no water to soften my fall. My body built up quite a bit of speed as I plummeted those thirty feet. My head crashed into a ten-foot-long boulder with such force that my sunglasses exploded into a shower of fragments around me. The impact bounced me backward like a ragdoll, smacking the back of my head with a crack. I had numerous broken bones in my face, a badly broken right wrist, and multiple other injuries. I lost consciousness nearly immediately and lay dying on the desert floor of Red Rock Canyon.

Why did this happen? Why did I end up surviving when I

should have died? Why did I survive while others die from similar tragedies? I don't know, but I am convinced of a couple of things. First, it was not God's will or actions that caused me to fall off the cliff. I believe God is love, and love is good and does no harm. The trauma of falling so far and hard that I should have died was not good for my family, friends, or me. The Creator of everything is assuredly beyond my comprehension, but that doesn't mean the Divine's and my understandings of goodness are of different natures or kinds. It means God's goodness is better and bigger than I can comprehend.

Second, as I hope to show in the following pages, although God doesn't micromanage the universe and directly cause everything that happens, Jesus does and will bring good from our successes, tragedies, and everything in between. One could even say that is the message of the cross and Easter Sunday. God took the worst thing ever-Christ being killed on a cross-and turned it into something amazing: the defeat of sin and death. The questions are these: Will we open ourselves up to receiving and seeing the possibility of beauty coming from our darkest moments and deeds? Will we surrender and allow ourselves to fall into love?

2

Warheads and Princesses

You're familiar with the old written law "Love your friend" and its unwritten companion, "Hate your enemy." I'm challenging that. I'm telling you to love your enemies. Let them bring out the best in you, not the worst. When someone gives you a hard time, respond with the energies of prayer because then you are working out of your true self, your God-created self. This is what God does. He gives his best—the sun to warm and the rain to nourish—to everyone: the good and bad, the nice and nasty. If all you do is love the lovable, do you expect a bonus? Anybody can do that. If you simply say hello to those who greet you, do you expect a medal? Any run-of-the-mill sinner does that. (Matthew 5:43–47 The Message)

So I can give you a more complete picture, let's temporarily press pause on me lying dying on the floor of Red Rock Canyon. Let's go back to five months before the accident. At the time, my job as an officer had me working as an instructor in one of the most advanced training exercises for the US Air Force. Specifically, it was the Mission Employment Phase (ME for short) of the United States Air Force Weapons School. The Weapons School is a five-and-a-half-month course that grants the equivalent of a graduate degree in war fighting. For over fifty years, the Weapons School has taught, trained, and equipped US airmen to form the most capable air force in the world.

ME is the graduation exercise for the Weapons School program. Over a two- to three-day period, students and instructors plan a mission, fly the mission, and then debrief how it went and ways to improve next time. ME is a final exam of sorts, the culmination of a long, rigorous training program. Students begin the course in academics about the fundamentals of airpower, enemy weapons, friendly systems, and basic tactics. They then focus for a couple of months on mastering their particular aircraft or specialty. Around the fourth month of the program, the students begin working together in small numbers of different platforms, including ten or so total aircraft. In ME, students are asked to put together all they've been taught in order to fly and operate the full spectrum of weapons available to the air force.

On this particular day in early June 2008, I was teaching Alex (who went by the call sign Thug) and Candi (call sign Sticki). Our specific job in the air force was to fly as electronic warfare officers (EWOs). Approximately seventy-five planes were scheduled to fly a mission simulating the buildup to and initial round of a war. This particular event was Thug's and Sticki's time in the limelight. The focus of the mission was to attack and exploit the adversary forces via nonkinetic means, which basically means to assault, confuse, and exploit the bad guys without blowing things up (which would be kinetic means).

Wide awake despite operating on the usual four or so hours of sleep for a Weapons School student, Thug's job was to command the overall planning efforts, putting everything a few other instructors and myself had taught him during the course to the test. While I took notes on what Sticki and Thug did in order to debrief them later, highlighting what they did well versus what they could improve, he confidently commanded the room, leading the other students in developing complex plans.

"What if the enemy fighters come attack us?" asked one student.

"Our fighters will press forward, and the large, less defendable aircraft will move back," Thug replied.

"How do we locate their most capable surface-to-air missiles, so we can destroy it before it shoots down any of our planes?" queried a pilot.

Sticki replied by explaining how one aircraft would pick up its radar and get a general location before passing the information on to a different plane—a jet that could pinpoint the missile's location from a safe distance by visually identifying the missiles or the nearby radar.

During small breaks in the nine-hour planning process, I passed important nuggets for consideration to Sticki and Thug. "How will you get the enemy to turn on the radar for that important missile when they know it will help us find them?" I offered.

Thug and Sticki orchestrated a strategy that kicked off with computer experts hacking into the enemy's military computer network and using US airborne collection assets to identify, monitor, and locate bad guys. Meanwhile, friendly fighter aircraft took up positions to defend our large, nonkinetic-focused planes (like mine!) because they had little in the way of self-protection. Shortly after this phase, Sticki coordinated for the EC-130H, a modified cargo plane with four propellers on it, which she, Thug, and I flew on, to begin attacking the adversary. Our plane would find enemy communications and radars and throw noise on their frequencies to try and prevent them from communicating or detecting friendly aircraft.

Partway through the planning process, I took a short break to call Lara, part of our nightly father-daughter ritual. "What did you do today?" I said to kick off the conversation with my little girl, who brought a smile to every cell of my being.

Lara described the highlights of her day, like how her mom and her watched a Disney princess movie. She went on to detail whatever she enjoyed eating that day, most likely something along the lines of chicken nuggets or fries. It was always nice to talk to my daughter, but this conversation seemed more important. Lara typically stayed with me every weekend, but during ME we worked seven days a week, so Lara and I had to rely on our phone conversations for all our connecting.

I got the usual four or five minutes of back-and-forth out of Lara before she ran out of steam. With my batteries recharged, I went back to strategizing with my military brothers and sisters. The day revolved around ideas for how to most effectively employ our US military assets while also estimating and planning responses to what we thought were the probable and possible enemy actions and reactions. We took very seriously Sun Tzu's axiom that we must know our enemy.

"We can place our F-15s at this spot in the north," explained one student as he pointed to the map.

"But what if the adversary's main surface-to-air missile is closer than we think it is and can shoot our fighters?" ventured another.

Multiple times during the day, colonels and generals stopped in to listen to Thug, Sticki, and the other students' ideas and strategies. They nodded in thoughtful approval, and I beamed with pride at jobs well done by my pupils.

Can a job get any better than this? I thought. *I get to help teach these soldiers to develop strategies, think through their opponent's responses, and then execute the mission.* In other words, I got to do two things I loved doing for a living, playing war games and flying!

Overall, that ME featured a week and a half of planning, executing, and debriefing missions. Following the exercise, graduation events were all that stood between the instructors and three weeks of vacation or minimum working before the next Weapons School class began. I loved my job, but after months of hard work, I looked forward to the rest and relaxation of "summer vacation." The first important thing on my agenda in the summer of 2008 was spending time with Lara.

Like usual, I woke up Saturday morning and went for a long run, approximately sixteen miles, while listening to books and sermons on my iPod. After cleaning up, I walked a few apartment buildings to the north of mine and picked up Lara. I scooped up my fair-haired, slender girl, who was full of giggles and smiles as soon as the door opened. We had a usual weekend routine that we typically stuck to. First up, a jaunt out of the apartment complex, around a Walmart, and across its parking lot to the local Starbucks. I am from the Pacific Northwest, so for me, daily coffee was akin to one of the major food groups. I was obsessed with mochas but kept the caffeine away from Lara, instead letting her pick a flavor for steamed milk.

Following coffee and lunch, we ventured off to the "Dinosaur Park" (a massive local playground) so Lara could play in the hundred-degree, not-a-cloud-in-the-sky weather. At the playground, there was a giant, fake dinosaur head that stood at the fore of a thirty feet by thirty feed sandpit that kids roamed around, chased each other through, and dug in. After spending some time in the sand, Lara raced over to twin, two-story towers that each had three slides twirling out their sides. Up and down she raced and slid over and over, as I tried to find a good spot in the shade from which I could stay relatively cool yet still keep an eye on her.

After an hour or so, we drove back to the apartments to spend some time cooling off in one of the complex's many swimming pools; there were at least six. Lara and I decked her out with pink arm-floaties, a pink swimsuit, and goggles. We made the two-minute trek to the pool as I carried her inflatable purple dragon and floating air mat. I hopped into the pool before stretching out my arms to await Lara's gleeful jump into the water. As she propelled her little body through the water, I chased her around, pretending to be a semiscary monster from the deep that liked to snack on, but never actually caught, little princesses.

Eventually, a smile came to Lara's face to butter me up. "Daddy, can we do the standing thing?"

"Sure," I answered.

While Lara treaded water, I moved into position behind her, placing my hands beneath her feet. She straightened her legs, and I lifted her out of the water with my arms extended. Lara thrust her arms into the air in delight as she stood on my hands, a foot or two above the water. When her weight shifted, I would move around to try and keep her balanced, until thirty seconds or so later, we lost our synchronization, and she splashed into the water.

"Can we do it again, please?" were the first words out of her mouth. We repeated the process for five to ten minutes. After finishing our water fun, we journeyed back to my two-bedroom apartment, strategically placed alone with no adjoining neighbors and above four garages, for Lara's naptime. I seized this opportunity to study for the master's degree I was pursuing at the time. My major was in ancient history, with a particular interest in the Spartans (before the movie *300* made them famous), a people who strongly believed in a particular way of life and relentlessly pursued it.

Sunday, Lara and I drove thirty minutes from North Las Vegas to the middle of the city to go to Valley Bible Fellowship (VBF) in my relentless pursuit of Jesus. That Sunday, June 15, the pastor spoke about reenergizing our relationship with God, a reality this church had helped accomplish in my life. I had lived my whole life as a Christian, but VBF had become a part of showing me what it meant to follow Christ not out of fear of going to hell or in accordance with a list of dos and don'ts from God. Instead, VBF showed me the power of loving others, feeding them, clothing them, and getting to know them. This love for and from others led me to a much closer relationship with God and gave me a far deeper love for our Creator.

A different way of saying this is VBF was part of me coming to understand that God wants to bring heaven crashing into earth here and now. That week's sermon highlighted Matthew 6:19–21 and the importance of relentlessly treasuring and pursuing God. "Do not store up for yourselves treasures on earth, where moth and rust destroy … But store up for yourselves treasures in heaven … for where your treasure is, there your heart will be also" (New American Standard Version).

The only problem with growing closer to Jesus, letting God's love transform me, and cultivating an increasing love for others was the job I loved, valued, and found worth in. Jesus's words, actions, and emphasis on loving *everyone*, including and especially our enemies, were working on and in my soul. The extravagant love God showered upon me was leading me to begin to love my enemies. For instance, I began empathizing some with terrorists. *I think I'd be pretty upset if a foreign nation had military bases in my country, used and controlled my people for our oil, and manipulated (and at times coerced) our nation's leaders, politics, and polices.* The seeds of desiring goodness even for Al Qaeda and people like Osama bin Laden were springing up in my heart.

For the previous couple of years, I had really resonated with the thinking, theology, and lifestyle of author and pastor Greg Boyd. One of his main points of emphasis was that nonviolence is a unique and key element of what it means to follow Christ. While drinking my nightly mocha, I sat reading one of his blogs on nonviolence and loving our enemies. As I read, I nodded in agreement. I saw in this way of being the good and beautiful lifestyle of Jesus modeled and invites us to. Our "enemies" have princesses like my daughter, and they have mothers and fathers who love them; we're not so different. Then, a small light bulb went off in my head. *Are wars and fighting in the Middle East or elsewhere (i.e., my job) compatible with me loving my enemy?* I wondered. *Well, I don't actually drop bombs or shoot missiles at them; I just jam their communications and radars.* I paused and processed my thoughts for a moment. *Which, of course, helps the other friendly forces I'm working with kill them. Hmm ... I'm not sure, but I have a hunch that even jamming their communications might not be compatible with loving my enemies.*

At this point, I resorted to bargaining with God. *Okay, Lord*, I began. *I totally get that loving everyone, including my enemies, is super important. I totally want to; I even feel the desire to in my heart. And I get that directly harming or killing them is not love. However, I'm a little fuzzy on the collecting and jamming their communications and* radars part. So because I have only eleven years to go until retirement, and Lord, you know that retirement from the military is a sweet deal, can we agree jamming my enemies is okay? Or at least leave me a little unclear on what I think about it?

3

The Wink

This mystery has been kept in the dark for a long time, but now it's out in the open. God wanted everyone, not just Jews, to know this rich and glorious secret inside and out, regardless of their background, regardless of their religious standing. The mystery in a nutshell is just this: Christ is in you, so therefore you can look forward to sharing in God's glory. It's that simple. That is the substance of our Message. (Colossians 1:26–27 The Message)

As the summer before my accident progressed, I came to one of my favorite parts of the Weapons School's three-week "summer vacation." Lara and I got to go home to Bremerton, Washington, for a couple of weeks. We cherished and looked forward to this time we got to spend with our family. On this particular vacation, we went and stayed with my sister, Leia, and brother-in-law, Erick. I always considered it great to go home and spend time with the family, but this summer was unique. I had a girl in the back of my mind.

Erick's sister was Kate, and we'd seen each other now and then at family gatherings over the years. The previous Christmas in particular, we had both hung out at Leia and Erick's house a couple of times, playing Wii and games, watching TV, and goofing off. Amid the general, communal good times, I'd noticed a spark between us.

With that in mind, on my trip home that June, I found myself thinking about how I had noticed Kate the previous Christmas like never before. For instance, as we played *The Home Run Derby* on the Wii, Erick, athletic and coordinated, swung and missed at a super easy to hit ball, at which point someone said, "Erick, I thought you were a jock. How did you totally whiff at that pitch right down the middle of the plate?" Some people chuckled and others did not. Kate and I laughed like it was the funniest thing ever. What was more, as our bellies rolled, we looked across the room at each other and seemed to hold each other's gaze for a fraction of a second longer than normal. If that had only happened once, I'd likely have thought nothing of it, but because similar moments occurred several times, I found myself thinking, *I wonder if there is something to those shared looks and laughs?*

In the latter part of June, Leia, Erick, their kids, and I were driving in their van to their friends' house for a birthday party. While sitting in the front seat next to Erick, I said, "We should have some adult hangout time after the kids go to bed. Maybe we could play cards."

Erick nodded. "Sounds good. I'll talk to Leia about it."

I hesitated for a moment, weighed the risk, and then ventured into the unknown by adding that maybe we could invite his sister. Erick smiled and said that sounded like a good plan.

I had not even seen her on this trip, but Kate started moving from the back of my mind to the forefront. The next day, I tried to casually bring Kate up to Erick again. "Have you invited her to come play cards on Friday yet?"

He told me not to worry and that he was all over it. Friday arrived, and I found myself wondering how I would know whether or not I should ask her out. We sat around the table playing Spades. Kate was not familiar with the game but grasped it quickly. At the time, I was pretty competitive and typically enjoyed winning games, so to express my interest, I chose to let her win a few hands so she would get the number of tricks she bid. Ridiculous, right? Kate noticed. "Thank you, Lang, but you don't have to help me win." I smiled in that "What are you talking about?" way, but I was busted.

There were more shared moments of laughter and glances during the evening, but all too soon, the game ended, and Kate went home. *So, do you want to ask her out?* I asked myself. As I thought it over, I tallied up some of her qualities that made her attractive to me. Spades is not a terribly complex game, yet she impressed me by not only catching on rapidly but grasping the subtleties of the game. Kate knew that sometimes even when she could win a hand, it was best to let Leia take it in order to better set herself up for winning two hands later.

What was more, talking to her was easy, not forced or uncomfortable. Conversation with Kate seemed a lot like having coffee with my dear friend Matt. Our interaction had a natural ebb and flow to it, we effortlessly engaged on multiple subjects, and the inevitable conversational pauses weren't awkward at all.

Physical fitness was important to me, and looking at Kate (I made sure to sneak some covert glances) told me it was a priority for her too. As I went for my daily morning run, where I tend to do my best thinking, I reflected on how she was smart, was easy to connect with, had an athletic build, looked at me with captivating eyes, and laughed at my jokes. Then I pictured her lips, which were full, soft looking, and quick to smile. *I'd like to kiss her,* I concluded. At that moment, what the desire for a kiss symbolized—mental, physical, and spiritual attraction—let me know I wanted to ask her out.

Later that morning, during breakfast, I made my next move through Leia. "Hey, sis, you want to play cards again tonight … and invite Kate over?"

"Sure." She laughed and grinned as she picked up the phone and dialed.

The second night, the smiles got wider, I brushed against her in passing, and it sent thrills down my spine. *Is there a way I can tell her I think she's smart and pretty, I want to get to know her better, and I'd like to kiss her—without really saying all that and being totally awkward?* I thought to myself. No conscious answer came, but somehow my mind and body instinctively knew what to do. As we played cards, Leia and Erick looked down or away from Kate and me for a second, so I seized my opportunity. We caught each other's eyes, and I winked. One deliberate bat of the eye communicated everything I desired, though I still needed to make my interest official.

The next day, Leia and Erick took Devin and Riley (their sons; they later added Ethan to the mix) along with Kate, Leif, Lara, and me down to the Fountain Park. By the ferry dock in Bremerton, there are multiple replicas of submarine towers sitting in shallow pools of water that kids run around and play in. Every few minutes, fountains go off and water erupts from the top of the towers, cascading down on the delighted kids.

While Erick played catch with Leif, Kate sat apart with her feet dangling in a pool. I knew that was my chance, so I walked over and sat next to her. We exchanged a few pleasantries before I dove into what I was really after.

"Kate, how come your brother never told me he had such a cool sister?" I smoothly remarked.

She chuckled, which I took as a good sign—certainly enough to move on. "I'm leaving tomorrow to go back to Las Vegas, but if I came back in three weeks for Devin's birthday party, would you go on a date with me?"

Her yes was sweet and life-changing. Later that day, I got Kate's phone number so we could start getting to know each other better. I read somewhere that a guy should not be too eager when courting a lady. With that in mind, I left Bremerton on Monday and did not call Kate until Tuesday, patting myself on the back for totally playing it cool.

From that day on, we talked every night. On workdays, I got home around 6:30 or 7:00 p.m. and ate dinner. Then I brewed up a massive mocha to drink while I surfed sports, computer game news, and some Christian blogs on the Internet before settling into reading or writing a paper for my master's degree. Around 8:45, I would begin counting the minutes down until it got to 9:00 and what became our nightly long-distance date over the phone. We talked for two or three hours each night. Topics ranged all over the place, from God to politics (there was a presidential election that year) to school to work. We shared our visions of our future relating to jobs, school, and places to live. We talked about places we'd like to vacation; we both dreamed of one day going to Greece as well as Australia. Kate and I spent long hours detailing what we thought it looks like to follow Jesus with our entire hearts and souls.

Two weeks into our getting to know each other, and one week before our planned first date, we were on the phone in one of our late-night chats on a Friday when I suddenly thought, *I wonder how much it would be to fly her down here tomorrow?* I checked and talked to her about the possibility, and within thirty minutes, this random thought had turned into, "So, Kate, I got you a ticket to fly down here tomorrow at 6:00 a.m."

At that point, I would say this was the most spontaneous thing I had done in my life, and it was well worth it. Remember how I knew I wanted to date Kate when I realized I wanted to kiss her? Once her visit was set, I immediately started thinking, *How should I go about our first kiss?* I wanted it to be memorable and developed several options. Like in the movies, I pictured meeting her at the airport, spotting each other across the crowds of people, and swiftly (but in slow motion) making our way into each other's arms as our lips came together for the first time at that moment. True story! I also imagined waiting until we got back to the car and leaning across the seats for a peck. What really happened was not as Hollywood as my first idea, but it created a good memory.

I brought Kate back to my apartment and gave her a quick tour of the place. To conclude the exploration, we went onto my small balcony. My apartment was at the south edge of the complex and gazed out over a nearby highway, so no buildings impeded the view. While standing there on a warm, clear July morning, we could see the entire city of Las Vegas stretch out in front of us. My arms sought

Kate, and I discovered I was right about her lips: they were soft and wonderfully full.

Our relationship flourished and grew as we got to know each other. I think that talking on the phone so frequently and for so long allowed us to quickly become intimate with each other's thoughts and feelings. In what was for me a moment of liberation, we shared our darkest secrets over the phone. I told her in detail what I had only briefly alluded to with a couple other people. For years I had been addicted to Internet pornography and riddled with shame for viewing women in such an objectifying and derogatory manner, feeling I'd let God down and had betrayed my ex-wife's trust. The deep shame had made me feel terrible for what I did, so over the years, I had vowed not to do it again over and over and over, but the weight of the shame kept me trapped in the clutches of Internet porn. My image of God didn't help either because virtually every day I would picture our Creator shaking the Divine head in disgust and anger at me. It wasn't until I finally realized that first, foremost, always, and no matter what, God loves you and me exactly how we are, that I became "freed" from the clutches of porn and the resultant shame. (I put *freed* in quotes because although I haven't looked at it in years, the temptation is still there, just much less than it used to be). With all that in mind, getting to share this struggle in full for the first time with Kate was a freeing act that lifted a huge weight off my soul.

We agreed in so many aspects of life that it was apparent we were extremely compatible, yet we disagreed in enough to make us complimentary. We both concluded our kids were very important in our lives and affirmed that following Christ included caring for people in need via food, clothes, and other loving acts. That said, in the presidential election, Kate voted for McCain, and I chose Ron Paul. Our political disagreement didn't create tension; instead, it sparked good conversations, not to mention that Kate having her own beliefs and opinions was very attractive to me.

As long and wonderful as our talks on the phone were, we both wanted more. With that in mind, at the end of September, I was scheduled to go to Alaska for a three-week exercise with the air force on a Sunday. The flight from Las Vegas to Alaska had a layover in Seattle, so I arranged to have roughly seven hours in between arriving and departing. I told Kate about this, and we made plans to have lunch and spend some time together in Seattle. However, I later secretly made arrangements to fly up Friday afternoon with Lara and surprise Kate, all with the intent to ask her to marry me that weekend.

In preparing for the trip, I showed Lara the half-carat diamond ring with a platinum bland and told her I was going to ask Kate to marry me. "But shh," I cautioned. "It's a secret." I probably should have known better than to tell a big secret involving a pretty ring to a three-year-old.

I let my family in on the plan too, so my dad picked us up at the airport and brought Lara and me to Kate's bank about forty minutes before closing time. In we walked, and Kate's jaw dropped. We stayed for a while and met Kate's friends and employees before departing for Leia and Erick's house. I road with my dad, but Lara wanted to ride with Kate, so we drove separately. Not too long after settling into Kate's car and getting on the road, my daughter blurted out something to the effect of, "You should see the sparkly ring my daddy got you."

Kate said, "Are you supposed to tell me that?"

"No, it's a secret," Lara answered.

Saturday was the day I planned to ask Kate the big question. Because our kids were very important to both of us, I wanted to do something unique and include both of them in the plan. We went to her son Leif's soccer match before a two-hour drive to a destination I kept secret until we arrived. I took her to a park with falls, Marymere Falls, located near the Olympic Mountains on the peninsula in western Washington.

We pulled into the park's parking lot, right on the shore of Crescent Lake, which stretched for several miles in all directions. It was almost sixty degrees out with some clouds but a lot of sun. Our star's soft beams glinted off the lake's surface, which was surrounded by a forest of evergreen trees. Mountains capped in snow rose nearby, towering over the trees. We hiked for forty-five minutes or so up a well-cared-for trail, stopping to take pictures here and there. One tree was so big that Kate and Leif joined hands while facing the trunk and stretched their arms as wide as they would go, but they couldn't even reach around the front side!

Toward the end of the hike, we trekked uphill a little to view the falls, a stream of water several feet wide and nearly one hundred feet tall. After we spent a few minutes enjoying the sights and sounds, I had Lara ask Leif if she could be his sister, followed by asking Kate if she would be Lara's stepmom. Then I whipped out a poem to ask my wonderful girlfriend to be my beautiful fiancée, getting on one knee and the whole bit.

> I love the way you smile,
> And how we joke around.
> I dig your sexy voice,
> And our many talks on the phone.
>
> But I hate it when you're gone,
> And we are each alone.
> I'd love for you to be here,
> And together we'll walk along.
>
> I love you for you,
> And the brighter light we bring.
> So please, Kate, marry me.
> Say yes and take this ring.

"Yes!" she quickly answered. "Yes!" she repeated with misty eyes and a huge, love-struck grin. Kate later asked me why I chose that particular site for the proposal, and I said, "If you take the R and E off the end of Marymere, you get 'marry me.'" What can I say? I'm a hopeful romantic at heart!

This was less than two months before the accident, and in my mind, life had never been better. On top of an invigorated love for God, an intriguing and prestigious job, and a wonderful relationship with my daughter, I was engaged to a lady I was crazy about. More important, not only was life firing on all cylinders, but it seemed to me I was grounded in a solid and stable sense of my own identity and worth. At the core of this lay a confident belief that, like every other person in the world, I was loved and adored by God exactly as I was, but I also rejoiced and rested in the reality that on the rest of life's measuring sticks, I was doing great. Successful and high-profile career? Check! Making good money? Check! Close family? Check! Romantic connection? Check!

Yet the problem was, these weren't the places I was meant to find my identity and significance. Although they weren't "bad" sources to derive my worth and sense of self from, they ultimately let me down, as the passing things of our world always do. It is not because the things of this world and life are "bad" but because they're fleeting; our world is constantly changing.

In the yearslong aftermath of the accident, I was medically retired from the air force (loss of job, status, and money), at times I was separated from my daughter and/or family by distance or difference, and Kate's and my marriage ended in divorce. Although the circumstances behind the transitions, losses, and shifts in my life were unique, change is a constant for all humanity. We move on from, lose, or retire from our jobs; we experience periods of relational and/or physical distance from loved ones; our bodies experience illnesses, hurts, and age-related transitions; and we lose those closest to us via separation, breakup, divorce, death, or something else.

The thing is everything in this life is changing … except for the character of God, and that's the "mystery" Paul writes about in Colossians 1:26–27. "Christ is in you, so you therefore can look forward to sharing in God's glory" (Colossians 1:27b The Message).

The Christ, the animating energy behind the universe, is in us, will always be in us, will always love us, will always find us worthy, and is always shaping us into the image of Christlike beauty, and *this* is the identity in which we're meant to find ourselves and our security and worth. God names each and every one of us worth dying for on the cross, which means each and every one of us is of infinite value, and though I ceased being an air force officer and Kate's husband, this truth will never change.

Before the accident, I found a good chunk of my significance and self-worth in Christ, but quite a bit of it was still in the usual things of our world: job, status, wealth, family, and romance. Unfortunately, when the accident caused me to lose my job, status, and a chunk of my wealth, instead of reassigning those aspects of my identity and worth to Christ, in many ways I gave them to the closest and most present person in my life, Kate. Realizing we're imperfect humans and may not be able to find 100 percent of our self-worth and meaning in Christ, I also believe that's what we're made to do, and the truth God invites us to rest in. What is more, I have a hunch that this is one of the easiest, most unnoticed ways we can fall into idolatry. When I allow something or someone else to name and assign, or subtract, worth from myself, I'm placing her, him, or it in the role of God. God names you, me, and everyone else loved, children, part of the family, and worth Jesus dying for. When I allow the words or actions of anything or anyone else to replace or subtract from this truth, I'm idolizing him/her/it. This is precisely what I did to Kate while we were married, which I think ended up being my greatest contribution to our eventual divorce. I'm sorry, Kate. I'm sorry, God.

4

Dying and a Cry for Help

A hostile world! I call to God,
I cry to God to help me.
From his palace he hears my call;
my cry brings me right into his presence—
a private audience! (Psalm 18:6 The Message)

I do not remember any of my fall, the events immediately preceding it, or the two months after it. Conversely, to Kate, it all seemed to happen in slow motion, frame by frame, as I went off the ledge, fell through the air, hit the rocks below, and bounced backward like I was made out of rubber.

Kate told the kids not to look, and then she raced down to where I fell. She yelled for help and began praying this sweet prayer: "Lord God, please have mercy on Lang." She repeated it over and over again. I read about Kate saying this prayer in her journal nearly six months after the accident, and Kate asked me if I knew what it was from. I did. It was from a Mars Hill Bible Church (in Grand Rapids, Michigan) podcast in which Ed Dobson talked about prayer. He said that when you don't know what to pray for, perhaps the most loving thing you can request is: "God, have mercy on _____." I had recommended the podcast to Kate, and she had just listened to it about a week before the accident, so it was fresh on her mind.

As Kate descended, I came into her view. I was slumped like a ragdoll between the two boulders I had hit. I was folded in half, and my legs were over my head, which lay crookedly to the side. It looked like I had broken my neck. My right eye was out of its socket, lying on my face, and I had a baseball-sized bump on my forehead. There was blood coming out of my eyes, ears, nose, and mouth. Thinking I was dead, Kate stared at me, not knowing what to do. Then she noticed my stomach was moving, which meant I was breathing, which meant I was alive!

Kate then saw that some other people had begun making their way over to help and yelled, "Someone call an ambulance!" A woman shouted back that someone had called and that help was on the way. My lips were turning blue, and blood was bubbling from my nose and mouth; Kate thought maybe the awkward folding of my body was making breathing difficult.

"I don't know if I should move him!" she said.

At that moment, a tall woman with short, neatly trimmed dark hair, and who looked to be Kate's age, climbed the rock. Her name was Julie, and she happened to be an ICU respiratory therapist.

After looking at me and assessing the damage, Julie said, "Oh, God. This is bad. This is really bad."

"I know! I don't know if we should move him," Kate replied.

Julie responded by saying she thought it wasn't a good idea, fearing that movement would lead to or worsen any paralysis caused by the impact.

With this recommendation hanging in the air, Kate pointed out that at this stage, my whole face was turning blue, and my eyes looked like they were going to pop out of my head. Preferring paralysis to something worse, they agreed to carefully shift me around.

Around that point, a couple arrived to help; from their accents, they appeared to be vacationing from another country. Kate heard the gray-haired man and the woman with a ponytail and white shirt talking to each other in a language she couldn't understand but struck her as European. Julie asked the couple to hold my legs while she grasped my head. Kate reached under my armpits and lifted my upper body onto the rock behind me. This put my body in a V shape, my legs propped up on the rock in front of me at a forty-five-degree angle and my body resting on the rock behind, also at a forty-five-degree angle. The new position helped drain the blood away from my face, which was swelling beyond recognition.

Kate knelt down by my side to watch my breathing while Julie continued to hold my head.

"Help is on the way, and you're doing a great job," Julie told Kate. Then my breathing stopped.

Julie calmly used her fingers to close my nose and told Kate to give me mouth-to-mouth resuscitation. Kate put her lips around my blood-covered lips and blew over and over. My chest filled and rose up like a balloon. Following each breath of life from Kate to me, she would lean back, and I'd give a weak exhale, lips quivering and making a flapping sound. While she did this, Julie continued to plug my nose, offering Kate words of encouragement. After a few long minutes, my breath spurted back to life, seemingly averting a crisis. Breathing a sigh of relief, Kate stopped the mouth-to-mouth resuscitation and lowered her tear-filled eyes. She again began her prayer for mercy.

Julie watched me breathe in and out a few times before telling Kate, "You need to still breathe for him because his breathing is too shallow." Later, she explained my feeble breaths weren't deep enough to get the oxygen my body (especially my brain) needed. Without Julie's trained observation and direction, I could have easily lost more brain cells and sustained more internal damage due to oxygen deprivation ... or perhaps even worse!

Between repositioning my body, the mouth-to-mouth resuscitation, and the sweet and simple prayer, I believe Kate and Julie saved me, but in my mind, God had a hand in my survival too. I say this because although Kate's breath prevented me from perishing right then and there on the canyon floor, by earthly standards, I still should have died.

I'd often taken my little daughter, Lara, hiking at Red Rock Park before the accident. When Lara asked me what Red Rock Canyon was, I told her it was a beautiful park made by God. In her young mind, this got translated into "God lives at Red Rock." So Lara would say, "God lives at Red Rock." God does indeed live at Red Rock Canyon, and I think it showed in a powerful way that day.

While Kate and Julie worked at resuscitating me, the older European man held my torso off the ground. During Kate's second round of breathing for me, he got tired and went for a rest. Kate and his wife slid their lower bodies underneath me, in the crevice between the two rocks, to support my back. Moments after sitting down to rest, the European man passed out on the rock and started convulsing.

"God, you've got to be kidding me!" Julie exclaimed as she moved over to help him. At that moment, his eyes opened, and he sat up, perfectly fine. Julie then returned to holding my head and told Kate she didn't need to give me mouth-to-mouth resuscitation anymore.

I was still alive, but if that was to continue, I needed to get to a hospital soon. Kate continued to pray for mercy on me and added, "Lord, please let help get here soon."

Kate yelled out to the kids to tell them everything was going to be okay and reminded Leif to not let Lara look at me. By then, Julie's husband, Michael, was with the kids and watched over them while Kate and Julie worked together to keep me alive. He made sure they stayed out of view of the scene unfolding below. While they saw me slide off the edge and disappear, Lara did not have to see her broken and bleeding father because Michael kept them on the middle of the plateau where they couldn't spy me on the canyon floor. What is more, Leif heroically distracted her from the severity of the situation by playing tic-tac-toe with her.

At one point, I regained consciousness and began moving my arms and legs. Kate told me to be still because they were supporting my head and body and trying to keep me safe from further injury. Disoriented and in shock, I quickly became combative and began violently trying to dislodge my arms and legs from their grasp. The group of them was only barely able to keep me still. Confused and unable to see, I thought my daughter was holding my head and yelled at her to let go. While Kate and Julie tried to keep my limbs from flailing about, my fiancée had to repeatedly tell me to be still. At one point, I even began shouting out one of my favorite parenting techniques: "Lara, let me go. I'm going to count, and you'd better let go. One ... two ... three ..."

Upon hearing this from above—what can I say, I'm a loud talker—Lara added her voice to Kate's, saying, "Dada, be still!"

Six emergency medical technicians and firefighters from the park arrived at about the same time everyone could hear the helicopter approaching to take me to the hospital. The EMTs and firefighters began to stabilize me while rapidly asking Kate a ton of questions. "Does he have any allergies? What does he do? From where did he fall? Does he have any medical conditions we should know about?"

They injected me with a sedative to cease my thrashing about. "That hurts!" I screamed.

Kate and Julie were still in position around me and partially wedged under me, so an EMT had them put a neck brace on me. As the helicopter came closer, the EMTs asked Kate to slide out from under me so they could put me on a backboard for transportation. The helicopter landed, and I was quickly placed in its back before it lifted off.

Kate stood for a moment, not knowing what to do next, before rushing over to the kids. She gave them a big hug, telling them how much she loved them and explaining to Lara, "Your daddy had a big owie, and we have to go to the hospital to make sure the owie is fixed."

A fireman guided Kate and the kids to the fire truck while the helicopter landed not too far away in order to better stabilize me before the flight to the hospital. Kate saw Julie making her way toward them and so moved to meet her, hugging her tightly. Julie offered to drive them to the hospital, so they took seats in my car, noticing my mocha still next to the driver's seat. The helicopter lifted off again to get me to the hospital, and as Julie drove, Kate called my family to let them know about the accident. Amid tears and sobs, she related to my sister, Leia, the shocking tragedy that had befallen me, and then her phone died.

Crying out is an important aspect of prayer. It's an essential way we connect to both God and people. During the minutes I lay dying on the ground of Red Rock, which felt immeasurably long, Kate cried out over and over in various ways. She first gently cried out to the kids, then desperately to God, then loudly to strangers, next firmly to me, later tiredly to medical professionals, and finally tearfully to my sister. Only some of these pleas were directly and consciously spoken to God, but in the end, they were all also prayers to our Creator and Healer. I say this both because God is everywhere, hearing everything, and because the Divine answer usually comes via people.

I once read about a lady who prayed passionately concerning a coworker. "God," she said, "I'm convinced you don't want her to move away to that new place and job she's pursuing. She has an important and powerful purpose here she's better suited for, so please change her heart and let her know she should stay." Finally, after repeating this prayer for some time, God nudged her with the reminder she was part of the Body of Christ. In short, she realized perhaps she was the answer to her own prayer, meaning she should turn her monologue to God into a conversation with her coworker.

The beginning of the answer to Kate's prayer for me was much the same. God didn't wave a magic wand to revive me. The Source and Sustainer of all creation breathed life through Kate to resuscitate my dying body, worked through Julie and her medical expertise to help save my life and preserve my health, moved through the European couple to keep me stabilized, and operated through the EMTs to evaluate, prepare, and get me to the hospital. I'm convinced prayers are a powerful force for good in the world. God answers prayers, and usually the answer is people freely choosing to love and care for others of their own accord … like it was for me.

Along these lines, in John 17, it seems to me we see spirituality and science coming together. In Jesus's longest prayer to the Father, He asks for humans to be one, just as He and the Father are one.

When we do this, Jesus points out when we love each other as if there is no separation between us, then the whole world will know God is real. In short, the Christ both requests and invites us toward oneness and interconnectedness.

The crazy, cool thing is it seems to me more and more science is showing people, atoms, planets, and everything is interconnected. For instance, the physical phenomenon of quantum entanglement shows when particles are produced or interact in a manner that entangles them, what happens to one will affect the behavior of the other even when the distance between them is immense.

Relatedly, the human heart produces an electromagnetic field, which extends seven to twenty feet outside our physical bodies. The positivity or negativity of our thoughts and emotions help shape this field, and this energy impacts the moods of people around us. We can, and do, brighten other people's days without a word being spoken! What I'm getting at is I think Jesus invites us to mindfully live in a reality that's already true. We are all already interconnected with and greatly influence each other. Whether we call it prayer or good vibrations, our thoughts, words, and actions help or hurt those around us.

What's the line, then, between what "God does" versus what "we do" when it comes to answering prayer? I have no idea. Regardless, I think prayer is important because God is a relational being, and we're relational creatures.

To take this full circle back to the theme of crying out in this chapter, I believe great relationships require vulnerability and authenticity. It's hard for me to imagine a person being more real or exposed than when one pleas for help. Calling for aid swings the door wide open for God and others to love us while also drawing us into deeper, more intimate relationship. I believe this is why, over and over in the Bible, we see our Creator answering the cries of hurting, wounded, or oppressed people. Love hears those in need and moves toward them with a caring and compassionate embrace, just as God, friends, family, and strangers did for me at Red Rock Canyon.

5

I Made It to the Hospital, so Everything Should Be Okay ... Right?

"Relax, Daniel," he continued, "don't be afraid. From the moment you decided to humble yourself to receive understanding, your prayer was heard, and I set out to come to you. But I was waylaid by the angel-prince of the kingdom of Persia and was delayed for a good three weeks. But then Michael, one of the chief angel-princes, intervened to help me. I left him there with the prince of the kingdom of Persia. And now I'm here to help you understand what will eventually happen to your people. The vision has to do with what's ahead." (Daniel 10:12–14 The Message)

A little while after I arrived at the hospital, Kate, Julie, Leif, and Lara entered the trauma center at the University Medical Center in Las Vegas. A welcoming blonde lady named Pam, the resident social worker, met them almost immediately. She took them to the Quiet Room, gathered some information, and asked whom she could call and who could get the kids. Kate did not have my cell phone and had only met one of my coworkers in Las Vegas just once, meaning she had little to go on when it came to the names and numbers of my people in Vegas. She asked Pam to call family members she hadn't reached yet, plus Josh, my air force buddy she'd met, although she didn't know his last name. Pam told her she'd see what she could do and left for a short while.

No longer actively trying to save my life, get help, or tell others what happened, Kate was left largely alone with her thoughts. As her surge of adrenaline faded, the reality of my nearly dying and perhaps a future with me being significantly handicapped set in. Tears streamed from her eyes in rivers of release.

Pam returned and let Kate know they were taking me for surgery, and she could see me. As Pam went over the situation with Kate, she shattered my fiancée's assumptions. Kate figured that the scariest part of the accident was over; I'd survived the fall and we'd made it to the hospital, so the doctors would surely be able to heal me. Pam destroyed this illusion by gently saying, "Lang is probably going to die."

The two of them walked down a long and sterile white hallway and around the corner as Kate tried to make sense of this news. There I was, lying on a gurney. My head had become round like a basketball, and my eyes had grown so black and swollen that I did not look like a person. Kate spoke to Pam for a couple of minutes and noticed the surgeon, Dr. Franklin, was just down the hall, talking on the phone.

My sister, Leia, a resourceful lady, knew where I was and called the hospital to get more details as she got ready to fly down from Washington State to see me. She first talked to Pam and then got a hold of Dr. Franklin, a conversation Kate was now witnessing in the hall. The lead surgeon told Leia if she wanted to see her brother alive, she had to get there right away.

Dr. Franklin then approached Kate to talk to her, going over the nature and extent of my injuries. Kate was shocked and disoriented, so barely a word the surgeon said made any sense or stuck with her. All she had the capacity to grasp was the surgery should take two to three hours. Kate was never one to beat around the bush, so after he wrapped up his explanation, Kate asked for a cut-and-dry summary of the potential outcome. "Could he die during surgery?"

The surgeon nodded. "Yes."

While she stood there absorbing this reality, the hospital staff worked around me. A short while later, they wheeled me off, leaving her alone. Feeling lost in more ways than one, Kate noticed a doctor nearby, so she walked over and asked her, "Where should I go?"

The lady tenderly guided Kate to the waiting room, where Julie and the kids sat. With emotion hanging heavy in the room like a fogbank, the hospital chaplain arrived and prayed with everyone, asking God to help the surgeons heal me. Shortly thereafter, Amy, my ex-wife, reached the hospital. While Kate cried and kept shaking her head, saying, "I don't understand," Amy sat next to her and grasped her hand in comfort.

Pam came back and let Kate know that my mom, stepdad (Rick), dad, and grandma were all on their way from Washington. Moreover, she had somehow tracked down Josh, who was also en route. With some help having arrived and more on the way, Julie took her leave, hugging Kate goodbye. From that time on, Kate began calling Julie "Julie Angel" because the love and miraculously timed help she'd given me that day were angelic. Amy and Kate agreed there was no reason for the kids to stay any longer, so Amy graciously took Leif along with Lara back to her apartment.

Alone for the moment and caught in the uncertain and often unnerving in-between space of waiting, Kate prayed again and found peace in God. Her tears, worries, and fears were very real, but from the moment I fell, she felt comforted by God, held by God. She felt as if she was being squeezed tightly in a divine bear hug and told that everything was going to be all right. Her soul felt as if God was at work and that some way, somehow things were going to turn out well.

Around the time Amy left, Josh came to the hospital with his wife, Jen, and listened to Kate recount the accident. Soon after which, my dear friend Matt called and told Kate he, his wife (Ali), and Kevin (another close friend) would get there from Tucson in the morning.

Kate sat there feeling all the feels. While praying, she cried, despaired, hoped, ranted, trusted, doubted, and more until, an hour and a half after I was wheeled into surgery, a man in jeans and a Hawaiian shirt with slicked-back hair stood in front of her. He was my neurosurgeon, and he told Kate I was going to survive the night at least, music to her soul.

In his words, I was "extremely lucky to be alive" at that point but still far from surviving long-term.

My skull was fractured, he explained, but he had repaired it. Given the nature of my injury, he said the staff needed to pay close attention to me overall, but particularly to the swelling of my brain and pressure in my head. They had a device hooked up to me for the sole purpose of monitoring this pressure, called the intercranial pressure (ICP) machine, and had placed a chip in my head to monitor swelling. The neurosurgeon went on to say that I was in stable enough condition that Kate would be able to see me soon. As he wrapped up his report on my status and care, the last thing the neurosurgeon told Kate was to continue praying.

After a little more waiting, filled with phone calls to various friends and family, Pam came to the room and let Kate know she could see me. Kate asked Josh to come with her as Jen stayed in the waiting room; only two people were allowed in my room at a time. He gently clasped her hand and held it as they walked down the long, cold hallway to my room, the last one on the right.

There I lay, perfectly still, surrounded by tubes and with a cylinder sticking out of my head, called a bolt. Its purpose was to monitor the pressure in my head, which doctors feared could increase to dangerous levels. I also had a breathing tube keeping my body supplied with oxygen. Large swathes of the hair on my head were shaved off, and there were staples running from the top of my forehead to the back of my skull, beginning in the center and arching toward my right ear. Their job was to close up the long incision from my surgery. Finally, there were slits cut into my skin stretching out from each eye socket. These were necessary to reduce the swelling on my eyes and save as much of my vision as possible.

Misha, my nurse, explained to Kate that my condition was still serious; there had been massive head trauma. Yet they were hopeful for a recovery.

The staff kept me sedated for most of the first day in the hospital, waking me up several times to better assess my remaining injuries and potential for recovery. The first time they revived me, I tried to pull out my IV and breathing tube, which ironically, the staff deemed a good sign. Given I wasn't successful and thus did not worsen my already poor state, they considered this a positive thing because I was responsive and able to move all my limbs. Later in the day, I even started answering to commands, such as "raise your arms," and "squeeze your hands." That said, due to swelling and severe damage done to my eye socket, I was unable to open either eye. What was more, with the breathing tube in place, I was unable to talk. Still, even though I was unable to see or speak, the medical staff was encouraged by my cognition and actions, so they began to think I might survive after all.

Some of my family arrived around 11:00 p.m. that night, having quickly packed, bought tickets, driven a bit faster than legal, and gotten on the earliest possible flight. Kate broke down and began hugging each of them: Leia, Kathy (my mom), and Rick.

Then Kate's tear-filled eyes met Erick's as they walked toward each other. Her brother, and my sister's husband, buried her in his strong arms, lifting the pain from her and filling her soul with warmth while tears rained down her face. They embraced each other for a long moment, a respite that had Kate feeling as if everything was going to turn out all right.

Not long after the family reached the hospital, Josh noticed Kate still had blood and dirt on her skin and clothes from the accident. "Honey, you really should go take a shower. The family is here, and they can handle things for a bit," he gently encouraged her.

Kate took the advice but did not leave the hospital that day. She stayed through the night, sleeping a mere forty-five minutes in an uncomfortable waiting room chair, as thoughts about the traumatic day and prayers for me rattled around in her head.

The experts, the doctors, had thought I was going to die … yet I didn't. Why? Did God save me? Did their skill heal me? Did the love of my family and friends play a part? Why did I live when I should have died? Why do some people die when they should live? Although I can't profess to know the answers to any of these questions, I do have some thoughts to help make sense of things.

Years later, in sharing a bit of this story over some beers with friends one night, I said, "I believe God saved me."

To which a friend noted, "Do you really? How would that mesh with your view that God loves everyone equally and doesn't micromanage the universe, yet others die from similar and even less severe mishaps? Did God pick you to heal but not others?"

"Touché," I replied.

I'm still of a mind that God played an important part in my salvation, but I'd put it differently than I did to her. I believe that though God helped save me, so too did the doctors and staff, Julie, Kate, the love and prayers of family and friends, and more. I say this because I understand our world to be an immensely complex place, one where the events that transpire are influenced by the past and present actions of people, nature, spiritual forces, God, and more. For instance, think about all the factors that lead to a traffic accident occurring versus not occurring: the fatigue of the drivers, the conditions of the road, the tread of the tires, the breaking capability of the cars, the reflexes of the drivers, the drivers' mental states (perhaps preoccupied with work or a fight with a spouse), the visual acuity of the drivers, and many more. Changes to any one of these can result in an accident happening or not occurring.

In a similar manner, the story about the prophet Daniel and the angel in Daniel 10 is particularly telling because it shows how God heard and "answered" Daniel's prayer right from the start, but spiritual forces and battles kept the answer from arriving for more than twenty days. Even though it was God's will to get a message Daniel, the actions of others thwarted it. God loves and wills goodness, wholeness, and health for everyone, however humans, angels, demons, creation, or others can frustrate this desire. Which begs the question: If God is all-powerful and knows everything, why doesn't the Creator just push aside any interference and see the divine will for our goodness done?

I think the answer is both simple and complex. It's love. God is love, which is relational and communal by nature, meaning it creates space for others. This loving space God gives allows others to have an authentic say-so, which means we can make choices and act in ways that harmonize or conflict (and everything in between) with God's good desires for us and the world. After all, love isn't love if it isn't freely chosen, received, and responded to. In other words, God's love allows for free will, and it gives space to people, creation, and spiritual forces to each have their own vote on what happens in our world. It seems to me, in the Biblical text, historical records, and my experiences, that God consistently gives us freedom to choose.

God desires, and acts, to flood our lives and the world with goodness, wholeness, health, peace, joy, and love. Yet simultaneously, love means God's wishes, our choices, our prayers, the influences of spiritual forces, the workings of nature, the actions of animals, and more weave together in an infinitely complex tapestry to determine things like whether I lived or died. That's why I believe God played a part in saving me and also tried equally hard to save people who have and will die. After all, creation is relational, and relationships are immensely complex and nuanced. We are in the image of the God who is love, which means our world is a community of love and gives space for both health and hurt.

6

The Healing Power of Community

> After a few days, Jesus returned to Capernaum, and word got around that he was back home. A crowd gathered, jamming the entrance so no one could get in or out. He was teaching the Word. They brought a paraplegic to him, carried by four men. When they weren't able to get in because of the crowd, they removed part of the roof and lowered the paraplegic on his stretcher. Impressed by their bold belief, Jesus said to the paraplegic, "Son, I forgive your sins." (Mark 2:1–5 The Message)

More friends and family poured in on my second day in the hospital. My dad (Lee) and his mom (Grandma Seymour) showed up during the morning. Soon after, some close friends, Matt, Ali, and Kevin flew up from Tucson, Arizona, beginning their journey with a taste of the healing power of a loving community. The day of the accident, while they scrambled to get tickets to Vegas, they ran across a flight attendant from their church, who provided them with free airfare. That night, my Uncle Lawrence, who lived not too far from Baltimore at the time, also arrived. More military friends, like Karl, began to visit the hospital as Josh passed word of the event on to our network of friends in the air force. The message reached so far, so quickly that even fellow warriors from Iraq and Afghanistan were already calling to express their concern and well wishes. Pastor Doug and a couple of my friends from Valley Bible Fellowship also dropped by to express their support, give Kate hugs, and pray for me. Love's floodgates had opened to lavish everyone involved with its healing and nourishing energies in the form of an ocean of family, friends, coworkers, and more!

November 11 was an encouraging day for those who'd come to my side, as well as the hospital staff. Kate rarely left the room during visiting hours, so she happened to be present during one of the times the staff removed my sedation. As I came to, she stroked my hand and gently told me know how much she loved me. Although my face and eyes were too damaged for me to see who was by my side, I recognized the sound of Kate's voice and quickly smiled in response. I even tried to pull my breathing tube out again, expressing with gestures and facial expressions that it hurt.

Still, there were some causes for concern in the eyes of the doctors. Sensors showed that my brain swelling could still be a problem. Additionally, whenever I was awake, my blood pressure and heart rate elevated significantly more than they should.

In the midst of my still serious medical issues, problems of a more practical nature came to the attention of Kate and my family and friends. Kate and I were planning to get married on January 1, 2009, less than two months from the accident. Immediately following our honeymoon, I then had military orders to move from Las Vegas to Tucson. Kate and I had flown to Tucson in September, shopped around, found, and had an offer accepted on a home we were looking forward to living in. My purchase had closed four days before the accident, and in preparation for this, movers were scheduled to pack and ship my household goods later that week.

As my family and friends discussed the impact of my accident on this and other aspects of my "regular" life, Karl volunteered to take care of arranging the move. Weeks prior, when I'd filled out the forms for the movers, I put Kate as the alternate person responsible for my possessions, meaning aside from me, she was the only person who could oversee and release my home goods. Karl met the packers at the apartment and, thinking quickly, told them something like, "It says, Kate? That's odd, he meant Karl. Easy mistake to make."

While he handled the movers, my dad and Rick sorted through my stuff and set aside several boxes of clothes, computer gear, and favorite books and DVDs—theoretically the small batch of items I'd keep in my possession and take to Tucson in my car.

Because I was not going to be moving from Las Vegas anytime soon, Karl got my main household items put into storage to keep them safe. Given the plans before the accident, my apartment lease was due to expire, so he also took care of all the little but numerous and time-consuming details associated with leaving a residence—shutting off cable, ending Internet, stopping electricity, cleaning the place, and so on.

On November 12, the doctors were pleased enough with my progress that they removed the bolt and chip that monitored the swelling in my head. They also performed an MRI on my neck because they had not yet determined what damage it had sustained. The imaging showed broken bones and a torn ligament, but thankfully nothing that would require surgery.

The good news and moments that gladdened everyone's hearts kept coming later in my second full day in the hospital. In the evening, the staff removed my breathing tube. Before it came out, though, they warned my people as to what they should expect. I had suffered a severe traumatic brain injury (TBI), from which fifty thousand people in the United States die annually. TBI is broken into mild and severe cases, the former being a relatively common injury with 1.5 million people suffering from it every year. Events like car crashes, gunshots, falls, heart attacks, tumors, and strokes cause it. The professionals in the ICU were thus quite familiar with the malady. Severe TBI in particular damages the social functioning aspect of the brain. It effectively eliminates one's filter, which pretty much always, in the hospital staff's experience, led to a good deal of vulgarity. A "head patient," as they called us, with major brain trauma reacts with anger and hostility.

"We've seen these cases a lot," the staff explained. "Just so you know, the first words out of Lang's mouth will almost certainly include lots of the F-word."

After the breathing tube was gone, Kate sat by my side. Meanwhile, while lying in bed, I rocked back and forth, tilting forward toward my legs and then back, forward and then back, over and over again. Sitting still has never been a strong suit of mine.

"What are you doing, dear?" Kate asked.

"Please," I breathed, the first words out of my mouth in the hospital.

"What do you mean, *please?*" she asked while hospital staff members shook their heads in amazement.

"Please," I struggled to get out several more times. Finally, I managed to string together what I really wanted, "Please, let me stand."

"Heck, no!" Kate answered with a smile. "I love you very much, and don't want you to hurt yourself anymore."

"I love you," I said in return, filling Kate's heart with joy.

I was not completely without the anger issues the doctors had warned Kate about though; it simply took a different form than expected. Soon after expressing my love for my fiancée, I began moving my legs off the bed and trying to get my torso to sit up. Picture the awkward feebleness of a newborn deer.

Weak, barely able to move, and unsuccessful in my efforts, I began "yelling" to express my displeasure at the situation. "I'm mad," I growled like a baby grizzly bear.

Kate simply laughed and rejoiced that I was so active and aware. Not appreciating her amusement, I began kicking my legs up and down like a little kid expressing his displeasure.

While Rick watched on, Kate moved over, firmly placing her hands on my legs to halt my thrashing. She looked me in the eyes, and I glared back. "Don't kick me," she ordered.

Rick chimed in by adding that if I kicked Kate, she would probably kick me back.

"So?" I retorted.

Falling Into Love

My campaign to sit up or stand continued for a while, until a nurse or a doctor gave me some drugs to calm me down.

Each of these days, and over the coming weeks, Kate sat by my bed virtually every visiting hour, and at times during nonvisiting hours as well. (Shh, don't tell the hospital authorities!) Particularly in the early part of my stay in the hospital, a steady stream of visitors came from work, church, and my family and friends who'd flown into town, each filing into the room one at a time, where Kate would give them the latest news (only two people were allowed in my room simultaneously). After Friday evening, November 14, though, she had a discouraging update at the top of the list.

Just before 10:00 p.m. that night, the last batch of visitors cycled through and left my room, including my mom, dad, and Rick, as well as Tim and Jan (my former in-laws). After they were gone, the atmosphere of optimism they'd left behind turned stormy as I began struggling to breathe.

As if a switch had flipped, my inhales went from steady and rhythmic to rapid, shallow, and sporadic. As I fought to breathe, gurgling noises came sputtering from my lungs. It didn't take long for Nurse John to become so concerned with this development that he called Dr. Floyd to the room.

He tried using two different oxygen masks to ease my breathing, but they didn't work. I started getting upset, kicking and flailing about. Around 10:30, Dr. Floyd decided that they needed to put the breathing tube back in. They asked Kate and Leia to go to the waiting room for the next thirty minutes while they reinserted the tube.

Fearing the worst, Kate broke down in tears, sobbing and thinking over and over again that I was going to die. Leia clasped her hand, and together they prayed for God's mercy, healing, and comfort for me.

Even though I'd shown steady progress for a few days, there was still a chance I'd die, as well as a high probability my health and especially mental faculties would be significantly impaired.

Realizing this, my family and friends were shaken by this turn of events.

Matt, though no less troubled than the rest, had a different perspective. It was a positive one, which began with praising God I was still alive, and he went on to note a full recovery was still a possibility. In Matt's heart, he had this sense that God had great work for me to do. He shared he was reminded of a story about Jesus when a soldier walked up to Christ and said that his servant and friend was paralyzed and in great pain. Jesus told the man He could heal the servant. Humbly, the man replied, "Lord, I do not deserve to have you come under my roof. But just say the word, and my servant will be healed." At the word of Jesus, the servant was healed the very hour the man approached Him (Matthew 8:5–13) Matt, Kate, my family, and many friends prayed with the belief that God could heal me in the same way.

On Saturday, November 15, Kate showed up at what became her usual time, 9:00 a.m. From that point, she would usually have stayed with me, telling me "I love you," praying to God to "have mercy," and keeping visitors informed straight through lunch time. But on this day, the eye doctor asked her to leave for a while. He checked and stitched up the cuts going out from each of my eyes.

Kate got cleared back in the room around 11:00 and walked in on a welcome sight. My nurse, Donna, was in the middle of transferring me from the bed to a chair to sit, giving me some exercise and letting my lungs drain a bit at the same time.

"Kate, it's not a bad thing to need to put his breathing tube back in," Donna explained while she worked. "Lang's still doing well; he simply wasn't ready yet to have the tube out. He made it twelve hours breathing on his own—that's really encouraging." She added, "We'll try taking it out again in a couple of days. I think you should know though, that Lang will most likely get pneumonia. That is normal for head trauma patients who have the breathing tube in for more than twelve hours."

With her spirits lifted, Kate watched on while I sat in my chair for four hours, exceeding the goal of two hours Donna had set for me. I was sedated, so it was more like four hours of slumping in it, but it was a positive sign nonetheless.

Lara left that day for Washington with her grandparents on her mom Amy's side, Tim and Jan. We hadn't seen each other since the fateful day I'd plummeted off the cliff because family wanted her to remember me as her superhero dad and not the virtually unrecognizable and quite broken father I currently resembled, and we didn't see each other again until mid-February. Leif had already returned to Washington a day or two earlier, so Kate and I were both without our kids. As such, she began to worry about how she would balance taking care of me in the hospital while still being an attentive mother for Leif.

In the midst of ushering visitors to and from the room, Leia, fit, thin, brown-haired, and extremely photographic (I don't just say that because she's my sister; she pursued modeling at one point), greeted Kate with good news. "Guess what?" she said. "I can stay with you for two more weeks. Costco was very generous and let me have a chunk of time off. This way, you'll have some help and won't have to take care of everything yourself."

Kate hugged Leia and told her she was very grateful and happy things worked out that way.

After my four hours in the chair, Donna gently put me back in bed, where I slept peacefully. Visiting hours stopped from 2:00 to 4:00 p.m., but the staff let Kate stay back in the room. This meant she got me all to herself, not to mention some time to rest. During our alone times, such as this one, she talked to me, prayed, read me passages from the Bible, read my favorite books, played me Dave Matthews Band (my favorite band), and wrote in a journal to me. Because I don't remember any of this part of the story, Kate's journal for me has given me many of the pieces I'm using to weave together this tale.

Josh and Karl visited practically every day during my first week in the hospital. Early on, Josh told some of the hospital staff they should call me Kermit because that was my call sign and what most everyone I worked with in the military called me. Word quickly spread, and for almost my entire stay in the ICU, everyone called me Kermit. They even began referring to my room as "Kermit's room."

Around the fifteenth, Josh and Karl showed up with a gift. They know I'm a fan of all Seattle sports, so they arrived with a Seattle Sonics jersey for me. Not only that, but they each bought matching jerseys for themselves and committed to wearing them each day until I got better. As passionate fans of the New York and Washington DC sports, respectively, this was a big show of support on their parts.

The night of the fifteenth, Alicia, Karl's wife, made dinner for Kate, Leia, my dad, my mom, and Rick at their house. This was one of the first of a plethora of acts of generosity from family and friends during my lengthy stay in the ICU. For instance, many of the wives of my air force friends provided dinner for Kate, and whoever else was in town, every night or two. In acts of extravagant love, they typically brought Costco-sized dishes of pasta, lasagna, and the like, which was far too much food for Kate and whoever was with her to eat. She would often share the bounty with hospital staff, much to their delight. The kindness of my community was like an avalanche in that it swept everyone up in a tide of giving and gratitude.

On my first Sunday in the hospital, Nurse Eilyn came by in the morning for some physical therapy of sorts. She would ask me to perform a small task and see how I did.

"Wiggle your toes, please," she said. In response, I moved my toes back and forth.

"Can you squeeze my hand?" Eilyn requested. I squeezed her hand twice.

Kate then asked me to open my eyes, and I tried, but there was so much goopy liquid in them that I couldn't get my eyelids to budge. At that point, it had been nearly a week since I'd last opened my eyes at all. Can you imagine?

That night, Kate sat and held my hand for a while. She noticed I was uptight and anxious, so told me I should relax and lie down.

Obviously agitated, I kept insisting on sitting up, shaking my head at Kate.

"I'm sorry," she said, trying to let me know she understood my frustrations. I was in a mood, they say, so I paid her gestures of empathy no mind. Vexed by my physical limitations and injuries and over being confined to a hospital bed, I threw off her hand. Following that, I began banging my hands on the side of the bed and kicking my feet.

Saddened, Kate kept repeating, "I'm sorry, I'm sorry," yet her words and calm voice had no effect on me that night. I kept weakly ranting and raging over my situation, not expressing what I did want but definitely indicating I was not happy with the current situation, and I at least partially blamed Kate for not doing something about it. Unable to calm me down, and both physically and emotionally exhausted, she left that night, praying the next day would be better and deciding to turn her attention to a practical yet important matter.

A week after my accident, with my apartment vacated, Kate was looking for a place to stay in Vegas for however long I was in the hospital. Knowing this, she'd already begun putting feelers out to my air force and church friends. While sitting in my room that day, Kate happened to mention it in conversation with my nurse for the shift, Arlyn, who generously offered to open her home to my fiancée. In the end, Kate stayed at Julie's house (a coworker of mine), but Arlyn's sweet offer warmed Kate's heart and was indicative of the amazing kindness, generosity, and love that friends, coworkers, family, the hospital staff, and more showed me, Kate, and out-of-town visitors throughout my stay in the hospital.

In fact, I would argue my community's love was every bit as important in my journey toward survival and recovery as God's healing and the medical professionals' care were. Why? Because we are all connected. Take for instance John 17; here, Jesus's longest recorded prayer centers on asking that people be one just as the three persons of the Trinity are one. In other words, we don't live isolated and separate lives. Together, unique individuals form one greater whole, just as the distinct Father, Son, and Spirit form one united God. Our actions, attitudes, and energies affect those around us. Likewise, we are impacted by the deeds, mentalities, and vitalities of others. We are interconnected.

In Mark 2, the actions of a man's friends resulted in his healing. Early on in his three years of ministering to people, news of Jesus's healing power spread. As the Christ traveled from town to town, more and more people began anticipating His arrival. They wanted to see, hear, and experience this miracle worker.

The man I'm referencing from Mark 2, though, was a paraplegic, which meant when Jesus came to town, the man couldn't go see the healer by himself. His friends carried him to the rabbi, intent on seeing their buddy cured. When they arrived where the Messiah was teaching, though, much to their dismay, they discovered a large and thick crowd blocked them from getting into the house to see Jesus. Undeterred, they simply hoisted their ailing friend onto the home's roof, and from there they lowered him down to the Christ for healing. Can you imagine? You see, physically and literally the healing of this one person came via the efforts, planning, and perseverance of many. Jesus even says it is the friends' faith in action that made the man well physically, mentally, and spiritually (as we see with Jesus both forgiving his sins and restoring his body in Mark 2:1–12).

We see this truth play out in team sports all the time. There's a reason why coaches and players give fiery speeches before and during games to motivate the team because the collective attitude of the players affects the performance of the team. When players are fired up and motivated to play hard for one another, they generally perform much better than when they're frustrated by a mistake or focused on making themselves look good. One great, or terrible, play or moment can elevate or deflate the performance of an entire team for the rest of the game because we are connected; our mentalities affect one another.

The same relationship can also be seen in our energies. There's a reason why teams win more frequently when playing at home: the positive and excited energy of the fans invigorates their team. A similar phenomenon can be seen in interpersonal relationships. There was a guy at a church I once belonged to with a larger-than-life personality who greeted people with bear hugs. What was more, he would joyfully clap and roar "yay" whenever it was remotely fitting during a gathering. He frequently smiled and expressed genuine interest in how people were doing. The effect of his positivity and enthusiasm was tangible and noticeable; his way of being raised the energy of the entire room, spreading joy like a wildfire to anyone fortunate enough to be in his path.

These examples of our interconnectedness illustrate why I'm convinced my loving community of friends and family was instrumental in my survival and recovery. Their presence, prayers, positive thoughts, and loving actions, whether near or far, were healing. They passed their hopes for not only my survival but also my thriving onto and into each other and me. Family and friends met one another and me with encouraging words and actions, even on the darkest of days. This amazing community of love visited me nearly nonstop; brought food for Kate, Leia, and others; put family and friends up in their homes; moved me out of my apartment; and more. The loving actions, hopeful attitudes, and positive energies of my community of family and friends combined to form a vital part of my survival and healing.

I got to witness the life-changing power of love via a firsthand case study of sorts during a later phase of my recovery. Following my two months in the ICU in Las Vegas's University Medical Center, I went to the VA medical center in Palo Alto, California, for inpatient rehabilitation. (To this day, I enjoy mischievously referring to "my four months in rehab" to people who don't know anything about my accident.) I don't start remembering things again until after I left the ICU, and a good chunk of my recollection of rehab is somewhat foggy, but one thing that sticks out from my time in Palo Alto are the other patients.

I especially recall those who were both there when I arrived and remained when I left. A good number of them began their recovery with injuries less severe than mine or had less rehabilitation to do than I did. Yet as I prepared to leave the hospital, they were still there, and I wondered to myself why they remained when I was leaving. I noticed one glaring difference between their situation and mine. I'd never seen them with a family member or friend, whereas Kate was a loving presence to me virtually every day, and a good chunk of my family flew down to visit me in Palo Alto.

What was the difference in our rates of recovery? I think I rehabbed more quickly not through any effort of my own but because I was constantly surrounded by and connected to a loving community.

How beautiful is it that my former in-laws flew to Vegas from Washington state to see me in the hospital? How incredible is it that my coworker Karl took time from his packed schedule to join my two dads in moving me out of my apartment? How loving is it that my sister, Leia, took weeks from her job and family to be by my side, while also figuring out and taking on managing all my finances? How much hope and positivity did it communicate that Kate stayed with me for months while losing her job and home back in Washington? I consider having such an amazing community of friends and family to be one of the greatest possible blessings in life, and it's my fervent hope and prayer that everyone gets to experience and live in this type of community.

7

You Are What You Think

Celebrate God all day, every day. I mean, revel in him! Make it as clear as you can to all you meet that you're on their side, working with them and not against them. Help them see that the Master is about to arrive. He could show up any minute! Don't fret or worry. Instead of worrying, pray. Let petitions and praises shape your worries into prayers, letting God know your concerns. Before you know it, a sense of God's wholeness, everything coming together for good, will come and settle you down. It's wonderful what happens when Christ displaces worry at the center of your life. Summing it all up, friends, I'd say you'll do best by filling your minds and meditating on things true, noble, reputable, authentic, compelling, gracious—the best, not the worst; the beautiful, not the ugly; things to praise, not things to curse. Put into practice what you learned from me, what you heard and saw and realized. Do that, and God, who makes everything work together, will work you into his most excellent harmonies. (Philippians 4:4–9 The Message)

Like Kate, while my dad was in Las Vegas, he often stayed at the hospital all day, coming back to my bedside to visit me multiple times. On a Monday evening, he came into my room, sat by my side, and clasped my hand. While looking at me broken, swollen, and black and blue in my bed, he broke down in tears, barely able to say a word to me. With his heart aching at what had happened to his son, my dad could only keep from completely losing it for a few minutes before excusing himself.

Along with my mom, Kate wrote and placed Bible verses in my room, verses to remind us and everyone who came in the room that God is a Source of healing. These verses guided her conversations with our heavenly Parent on many nights. Perhaps coincidentally, or perhaps not, on the very same night, they mindfully penned and hung the Bible verses as visual prayers; my nurse's name was Prayer.

Beautifully, these words of inspiration and love were intended not just to lift the spirits of friends, family, and myself but also for the hospital staff and anyone else who happened to see them. They were visual icons of love meant to encourage everyone. Gesturing toward the verses one day, Kate told me in a conspiratorially whisper, "We are ministering to people all day, babe, and they don't even know it."

In looking back at the verses months later, this one especially stood out to me: "Fear not, for I am with you. Do not be dismayed. I am your God. I will strengthen you; I will help you; I will uphold you with my victorious right hand" (Isaiah 41:10 NIV) What I love about this verse is it doesn't give false hope. It doesn't promise that God will wave a magic wand and heal any ailment, nor does it put the onus on us and say God will help us if only we have enough faith, believe correctly, or pray well. Instead, to me the transformative power of this verse is it clearly communicates a game-changing truth: God is with us in and through everything life throws at us. Divine Love is truly always all around us. It's continuously by our side, holding our hands, and within our spirits filling us with life and hope. With the adoration of heaven on our team, not even death seems so scary.

While Kate and Leia were keeping me company that Monday night, they chatted with each other. In what had become their routine, after leaving the hospital for dinner, they came back and sat on either side of me, in the dark (so I could sleep, not because they were having a séance or something). An hour or so later, they busted out the dessert they'd brought that evening. I am a big fan of dessert, eating a bit of ice cream or cookies almost every night before the accident. Leia and Kate decided to eat dessert regularly in support of me, thinking doing something I took pleasure in, but was currently unable to enjoy, would be a loving way of expressing solidarity with and support of me. At least that was what they later told me.

Seriously, though, I think they ate the desserts as both an act of camaraderie and love for me, as well ase for their own pleasure. While they savored some yumminess that night, their conversation bounced from topic to topic until Leia suddenly declared, "We need to come up with a name for ourselves! You know, some catchy, cool, and meaningful title that describes our roles here at the hospital."

They spent a short time tossing around a few ideas before Kate came up with the clincher: "Bedside Warriors!" The ladies then continued their vigil until about 11:30 p.m., the normal time they left for the day.

The next morning, Kate began another tradition in my honor. She and Jen, my air force friend Josh's wife, ran three miles together as the sun was rising. Leia was excited by this idea and asked Kate if she could join the fun on November 19, just over a week after my accident.

When Kate arrived in the early part of the eighteenth, she found me sitting in a cardiac chair—a bad omen. These metal-framed devices are used for patients suffering from cardiac or respiratory problems. They're made to be easy to get patients in and out of, and by sitting me upright, the goal was to get the fluid in my lungs circulating. The reason for this, as Nurse Elizabeth let Kate know that morning, was they thought I had pneumonia, even though the first set of cultures came back negative.

Adding to Kate's sorrows a bit later was the word her wedding dress had been delivered to her house in Washington that day. A tear came to her eye when she realized that we were no longer going to get married on January 1, as we had planned, but she found hope in the thought that God had saved my life and we would still get married soon.

Then around midday, as if my probable pneumonia and the postponement of our wedding didn't combine for enough of a downer, a couple of air force safety investigators showed up to speak with Kate about the accident and surrounding events. It was just their job, and an important one at that, but what their task effectively called for was for Kate to relive the trauma of the accident by recounting it. Fortunately, Karl, tall and reassuringly solidly built, made sure to show up and provide Kate strength and moral support.

The investigators had Kate recount not only the accident itself in detail but also the seventy-two hours prior to it. The reason was they needed to check into any odd behaviors on my part, such as suicidal ideations, erratic behaviors, or irresponsible actions (like excessive drinking), which could have been related to the fall. Along those lines, they asked very detailed questions, such as wondering what I'd eaten for dinner the night before, what I'd drunk, and how much I'd drunk. Kate recounted how we'd eaten at the Cheesecake Factory, and I'd ordered the Thai Chicken Pasta and a Long Island Iced Tea, two of my favorites at the time.

That night, Leia and Kate went to Chili's for dinner; their chips and salsa were one of my fiancée's comfort foods. After the main course, in keeping with their plan to eat desserts to show solidarity with me, Kate and Leia tried one of my favorites, the Chocolate Chip Paradise Pie. After a couple bites, Kate frowned and asked, "Does this have coconut in it?"

"Yes," came the answer as Kate determined to not eat anymore. She can't stand coconuts. Apparently solidarity can only take you so far.

After the ladies returned to the hospital, Dustin, the fit (he later appeared on *American Ninja Warrior*) and energetic leader of the Bible study group I went to, came by for a visit. As he came to the door, he paused and gathered himself before coming in to check in on and encourage us. It was as if he was on the precipice of entering a foreign country. In fact, the first time he had visited the hospital, after walking into my room and looking at me, he nearly turned around and left. You see, he had thought he was in the wrong room because I was that unrecognizable.

This evening, Kate asked him if there was room for her to join the small group I'd been in, which there was. Even though I was sedated a good portion of the day, my recovery was going well enough that she figured she could go, bring the materials back to my room, and go over them with me.

"How is everything going for you?" Dustin asked.

"Pretty good," Kate replied, "My focus is on Lang. It is kind of hard for me because I'd only packed for a weekend stay. So, I don't have day-to-day supplies, extra clothes, and things like that."

Dustin nodded thoughtfully. This need took root in both his and his wife Hope's hearts.

The next day, Wednesday, I was wide awake when Kate came strolling through my doors. I gazed at her intently and gave a big grin. I attempted to talk repeatedly, but with the tube in, nothing could come out. It looked like I was trying to say "please" again as I scooted myself to the edge of the bed in an attempt to stand.

Kate took advantage of my increased awareness by asking some questions, which I responded to with head nods or shakes.

"Were you able to sleep last night?"

I shook my head no.

"Was it all the noise and constant poking and prodding?" Kate asked?

Yes, I nodded.

Of course, the "poking and prodding" wasn't bad; it was part and parcel to the medical staff's job of healing me. In line with that journey toward health, after Kate and my conversation, Dr. O (short for Ozobia), the attending physician, met with her to talk about my plastic surgery scheduled for the following day. He told her they were going to put a tracheotomy in before the operation, which meant the breathing tubes could be taken out in a few days. Cheerfully, this meant I'd be less uncomfortable, but sadly I still wouldn't be able to talk as they planned to wire my jaw shut. Even better news, however was that according to Dr. O, based on my recovery to that point, he estimated I would be able to leave the ICU for inpatient rehabilitation at another hospital in two to three weeks!

Later in the day, while Kate was hanging out in my room like usual, one of the nurses tried to get me to do some physical therapy by asking me to make some small movements. *Tried* was the operative word, as the following scene became a trend over the coming days.

"Kermit, can you put your thumb up, please?" she requested.

I did nothing.

Unperturbed by my lack of cooperation, she quickly followed this up by asking me to open my eyes.

Once again, I did not move a muscle.

But then a different voice reached my ears as Kate said: "Put your thumb up, please."

Up went my thumb as quickly as possible. Quite frequently the hospital staff would ask me to do a certain task, and I ignored them. Yet when Kate made the same request, I would carry it out. Apparently, even while lying in a hospital bed, I was trying to woo my fiancée and gain her favor! Either that or I was just being difficult.

The threat of pneumonia and postponement of the wedding aside, my recovery was going well. With Kate's help, the nurses were having me run through physical therapy routines to build my strength and coordination back up. Meanwhile, the doctors were moving on from urgent, life-saving procedures to less essential but still important tasks, like the upcoming plastic surgery and inserting metal scaffolding to set my broken right wrist. Likewise, my family, friends, and Kate were also transitioning from crisis mode to something of a routine, at least as much as regularly visiting and caring for a loved one who should have died in the hospital can be named *routine*.

Part of this new normal included regularly communicating my

ups and downs to the many family and friends who weren't in Vegas. It's amazing how rapidly and easily word spreads in our modern, networked, social-media-driven day and age. Within days if not hours of my accident, scores of kin and friends across the country and around the world had heard what happened. Friends from as far-flung places as Singapore, Iraq, Germany, and Afghanistan were praying for and thinking of me, and they were eager for news on how I was doing. Because Kate had her hands full encouraging me and updating hospital visitors, Matt devised a great way for her to spread the latest info, a blog, which she updated nearly daily. So many people became enthralled with this story of hope, love, and healing, there were nearly one thousand hits on the blog from November 19, some from people neither Kate nor I even knew.

As usual, on Thursday morning, November 20, Kate walked in at 9:00 a.m., as soon as visiting hours began. I opened my eyes and smiled at her, bringing an inner light to her eyes. Most of the time I was asleep, so it was a bit abnormal for me to be both unsedated and awake, as I was that morning. What wasn't infrequent, however, was my trying to get out of bed and stand up throughout her unusually short stay. I had a pretty one-track mind during my time in the hospital, and quite regularly whenever I was awake, I was trying or scheming to get out of bed and leave. My unsedated rebelliousness that morning was short-lived, though, because not long after she'd arrived, the doctors asked Kate to leave because they needed to prepare me for surgeries.

First on the schedule was a CAT scan to get an up-to-date image of my head, where the doctors were planning to spend three or more hours working. By the early afternoon, the pre-op procedures had begun in earnest. First, the doctors gave me a tracheotomy, putting a tube directly into the base of my throat to assist my breathing. This allowed them to remove the tube from my mouth, which I expressed great gratitude for following the operations. Finally, they cut a hole into my stomach to place another tube in my body. The feeding tube was necessary for pumping nutrients straight into my stomach because once it was fixed, they were going to wire my jaw shut so it could heal, which meant I wouldn't be able to eat.

After the staff's prep work was done, plastic surgery for my face became the main event for the day. There were a lot of broken bones to be repaired and work the doctors needed to do to make me look like me again. For instance, my jaw wasn't fully connected to the rest of my head, and my right eye socket was shattered. The extent of the broken bones and injuries to my head was so severe that the doctors said I had a "floating face," which pretty much summed up my cosmetic condition.

First, the hospital staff fixed my jaw, inserting titanium into the top part of my mouth by reshaping it to its original form. When done with that section, they wired my jaw shut for the next three weeks. This immobilized it and gave it time to set and heal.

Another main area of focus for the plastic surgery was my right eye socket, or orbit. The doctors had to completely reconstruct it because that spot had been one of the closest to my impact in the fall. My right eye and the surrounding area had suffered substantial trauma; if you recall, when Kate found me on the canyon floor, the eye was out of its socket. To give it a couple of days to recover after the surgery, the doctors poked a thread through my eyelid and sewed it shut. As with my jaw, the doctors used bits of titanium to piece my eye socket back together.

From there, they moved on to my right cheekbone and forehead. Some years later, in seeing an X-ray of my face, the glow and number of pieces of metal in my head reminded me of haphazardly placed lights on a Christmas tree. That said, unlike the unsuccessful efforts of "all the king's horses and all the king's men" in the Humpty Dumpty poem, the hospital's medical staff was able to put me back together again.

Everything went as planned, and Kate came back to visit me that evening. She noticed that I appeared much more peaceful after the surgery and repeatedly expressed how handsome I looked. Looking at my mouth, wired shut, she noted that the arrangement made my lips pucker, which led to her telling me she wanted to kiss me.

I lay in bed in restful slumber, and Kate talked to me as if we were carrying on a normal conversation. "You got a ton of cards with well-wishes and Starbucks gift cards from air force friends in Tucson," she told me. (That was my duty station before Las Vegas.) "Dear, you are so loved and admired by so many people. I am truly impressed and flattered that you chose me to love you."

She left that night happy that my healing seemed to be going really well and looking forward to departing the ICU for rehabilitation fairly soon. Her joy was particularly palpable that night because it looked like I'd go to the VA in Seattle, which would place Kate close to friends, family, and, most important her son.

When she came to see me the next morning, my legs were wiggling around but strapped down because, once again, I had been trying to get out of bed. "Good morning, sunshine!" she said brightly with the usual greeting Leia had come up with, and they both had adopted. I turned to her, opened my left eye, and smiled from ear to ear.

"Aww, my sweet man. I love you," Kate said in response.

Stretching toward her, I puckered my lips in her direction. She leaned down and kissed me, three times in total. Our first post-accident kiss left our cheeks flushed, toes tingling, and beaming to everyone like schoolkids after their first kiss. In my mind, it was like something from a Hollywood script, only there was no makeup, lighting, or music, and I looked like I'd been run over by a car twice and was hooked to a slew of machines making a cacophony of noises!

The kiss wasn't the only post-accident first that day. Michelle and Jerome, physical therapists, came to do some exercises with me. At first, they had me sit up. This led to a fit of coughing, which they told Kate was a good indication. I had a runny nose too and so kept wiping it off. As I sat and moved around, Kate and the therapists talked to me, and I smiled and smiled and gave them thumbs-up, a gesture that rapidly became my silent signal for happiness and contentment. I should note, however, that although my recovery was going well, I was still incredibly weak and in a sad state. For example, when I gave a thumbs-up, it was not at all what most would imagine. Instead of four fingers curled together and my thumb being clearly erect, the best I could manage was a slight parting of my thumb from my fingers.

The big news of that session, though, was this: Eleven days after the accident, Michelle and Jerome had me stand for the first time! For the most part, I managed the feat on my own, with some assistance from the therapists in balancing. As I stood there, I smiled widely at Kate and gave her a double thumbs-up. I could last for only a few minutes, but it was enough to fill my family's hearts with joy and optimism.

Kate summed up all their feelings in saying, "My heart is dancing right now."

The day kept getting better as Dr. O came and spoke to Kate about my leaving the ICU even sooner than he'd thought just days before. He said that if my recovery continued at its current rate, I would be cleared for transportation to Seattle as of Monday, November 24. The only thing that seemed to be holding me back was that air force approval hadn't come yet; they had to sign off on the transfer. Although the situation was looking good, I was still in pretty poor shape. In addition to only barely being able to move my thumbs and briefly stand with assistance, I had enough continuous pain that the staff put me on a constant morphine drip to dull the discomfort.

Speaking of pain, my new belly tube was a pain in my stomach. I kept grabbing at it, making it clear I wanted it removed or would pull it out myself.

"No, Lang," Kate said. "You need that tube to feed you."

I frowned and tried to say something to the effect of, "I don't care. It hurts, and I want it gone!"

"I love you," Kate replied. "I love you, I love you," she said over and over again. "I am just going to keep saying, 'I love you,' because you can't get mad at me if I keep saying, 'I love you.'"

"That's true," I mouthed as much as a person could with his mouth wired shut, to Kate's delight because she could make out what I was attempting to say.

Word about Kate, my family, and my friends' love and devotion for me, as well as my uncharacteristic lack of anger and profanity, had spread through the hospital's staff. This meant nurses, doctors, interns, therapists, and more would stop by the room to see us and say hi, even when they had no specific business in the area. For instance, one of the interns came in that day to encourage Kate. He told her he had gone through a similar injury, so he was confident I'd make it through. "Your presence is helping him do that," he added. "His family, friends, and you being a constant loving presence by his side is giving him hope."

A few years later, but before we got divorced, Kate introduced me to yoga. This practice was, and continues to be, a source of healing, transformation, and strengthening in my life. It not only makes a person physically and mentally stronger, but it helps connect a person's mind, body, and spirit.

An interesting phenomenon among yogis and other like-minded folks is the idea of manifesting. The thought is our minds are really powerful, so if you want something to be true, envision it, imagine it, meditate on it, believe it's going to happen, and name it, and it will come true. This can apply to a wide range of things, be it a new job, a pay raise, a house, finding a spouse, or being healed from a disease. This way of thinking isn't unique to the yoga community; in Christianity, it's called the Prosperity Gospel. Personally, I don't subscribe to these theories 100 percent, but I do believe they embody an important truth.

I think in a very real sense, we are what we think, or to put it a different way, I believe positive thinking has power and tangible benefits. Say, for instance, next week you are going to interview for a promotion. Now, imagine you believe you're terrible at interviews, and you're convinced you won't get the job. Over the week, you repeatedly think about these "truths," and in nearly every conversation you have with family and friends, you tell them how you're a horrible interviewee and just know you won't get the job. Conversely, imagine you think you're great at interviews and are confident you'll get the promotion. Further, you humbly express confidence in your abilities and the odds of you getting the job in talking to those close to you. Now, though neither mentality means you for sure will or won't get the job, without changing anything else, I'd say the version of you with a positive perspective has a much better chance of getting the promotion than the negative you.

What is more, I also think positive thinking has a contagious power to it. Again, imagine you're interviewing for a promotion next week. Now, consider what effect your friends would have on you if they universally express doubt you'll get the job, versus if they collectively say they think you rock and will get the promotion.

With this in mind, I'm convinced the near universal positivity, love, and support of my family and friends, both near and far, had a tangibly healing influence on me. It brings to mind the words of the Apostle Paul in Philippians. It's his most positive and joyful letter, yet he wrote it while sitting in prison (really more of a house arrest) and potentially awaiting a death sentence. He writes about how when we mindfully celebrate God and focus our thoughts, words, and actions on things that are positive, good, beautiful, and true, then the peace and calm of God will fill our souls ... even during times of trouble (Philippians 4:4–9).

The positivity of my family and friends lifted my spirits, brightened my days, and helped heal my body. What was more, their bright light of love amid the tragedy stood out to and attracted others. They were like a bug light to which all the mosquitoes, flies, and such were irresistibly drawn. The hospital staff and people across the country I didn't even know were attracted to my community's love, support, and hope. Instead of being killed on arrival, like the bugs, the positivity and love from my family and friends shot life into the hearts of others.

8

Laughing, Crying, and Everything in Between: Being Present to Ourselves and Others

Now Jesus wept. (John 11:35 The Message)

I've told you these things for a purpose: that my joy might be your joy, and your joy wholly mature. (John 15:11 The Message)

I came that they may have life, and have it abundantly. (John 10:10b New Revised Standard Version)

My recovery was going well, and my family and friends' light and love was a source of joy and life to not only me but others as well However, there was still a cost. Around this time, Kate realized the huge price of her continued presence in Vegas and at the hospital with me. She already missed her son Leif greatly and struggled with feeling like she wasn't fulfilling her motherly duties. Adding to that stress, she found out that she was losing her job. The little vacation time she had remaining was running out, and she didn't qualify for any medical or emergency leave because we weren't married yet. No job or income meant she could not make payments on her house. Furthermore, its monthly tab was so high that renting it out would not even come close to allowing her to make her mortgage, and selling it (although she did try) wasn't really an option because she'd bought at the height of the market, and with the market crashing that year, things were upside down as a result. She sat that night as the heavy reality of losing her home, something she'd worked years to save up toward, left a hollowness in her spirit.

Not only had she worked hard to buy this home, but it represented *way* more to Kate. As her first home, it was the fulfillment of a long-held dream, a symbol of arriving and succeeding in life. What was more, it stood for independence in that she'd managed to do it as a single working mom. Thus, with no small amount of sadness and loss, she declared to herself, "I don't care. Lang's way more important. And besides, it's just a house."

On Saturday, I spent the entire day off the ventilator, breathing on my own. While the respiratory therapist looked me over, Leia and Kate sat in the room chatting and listening to the radio in the background. As was often the case, they had the dial tuned to Air1. My therapist's ears perked up as he heard the radio, so he turned and asked them, "Are you Christian?"

"Yes, we are," they told him.

"Are you going to church tomorrow?" he asked in a manner that made it apparent he was going to invite them to his church if they didn't have their own.

"Yeah, in fact, we're going to Lang's church, Valley Bible Fellowship," Kate said.

The therapist smiled, "Wow, that's where I go too. I was going to invite you!"

As they spoke some more, he began to open up to Leia and Kate, as numerous other staff and visitors to the hospital had while I was a patient. "My brother is in the hospital because his heart stopped during hip surgery," my therapist explained with a sorrowful and worried look on his face. "I'm really worried about this near-death experience because he isn't a believer in God and Jesus."

"Wow. We're so sorry," Leia and Kate responded. "That's incredibly hard and scary. You're courageous for sharing that with us. Thank you! We'll definitely pray for you all."

Having shared his heart and struggles, the respiratory therapist smiled at their concern. Still worried, but with a noticeably lighter expression for having shared his burdens, he turned to finish checking up on me before departing for other duties. He left Leia and Kate with a silent thank-you and a positive update on my recovery.

Although I was improving and potentially nearing the end of my stay in the ICU, I was still suffering from the effects of a severe traumatic brain injury. That, combined with the amnesiac effects of drugs the hospital staff had me on, led me to frequently forget why I was in the hospital and to repeatedly try to escape. Pretty much whenever I had the opportunity and the energy, I would try to pull the tubes out of my body and stand up. Lord only knows what my plan of action after that would have been, but fortunately I never got that far.

Knowing my desire to escape, the hospital staff employed various measures to keep me comfortable, able to move appropriately, and unable to injure myself. For instance, they tried strapping my arms down, but my nurse, Jeffrey, didn't like that option. "A person should have his dignity and not be strapped down," he remarked.

Still, Jeffrey realized they needed to do something due to my insistence on moving around and pulling out/off my trach, splints, feeding tube, and even my robe! He started putting extremely large mittens on me. Their boxing glove shape was cumbersome enough to not let allow me get my fingers wrapped around the items of concern. Kate told me they looked like Mickey Mouse gloves.

After my short yet frustrating stint of being strapped down, I appreciated having some more freedom, but I didn't like the gloves either; they got in the way of my end goal, after all. I tried to get the mittens off as best I could. Apparently, the only method that came to mind was to try to bite them off. The problem was that my mouth was wired shut! As I sat there trying to bite my gloves off, my futile efforts sent Kate and Leia into peals of laughter.

Generally speaking, though, they didn't find my frequent attempts to scoot off the bed and stand up funny; they were worried

I'd hurt myself. Yet they managed to find some humor in the situation by giving me a nickname. My "Bedside Warriors" dubbed me Scooter. "Scooter, stop trying to scoot off the bed." The best part was that I started responding to the new moniker!

Sunday morning found Leia and Kate going to the church that had meant so much to me. "I'll probably be an emotional wreck, Leia," Kate warned my sister on the way to Valley Bible Fellowship. "Church already makes me emotional, but this whole situation will make it even more so."

They arrived and sat down, waiting for worship to begin, when Nathan, one of the guys from my small group, walked over and sat by them. He gave them comfort and made them feel not so alone. Pastor Doug swung by and talked to them for a few minutes as well, promising to come by the hospital on Monday with supplies for them. As the church service began, Kate kept expecting the tears to start falling any minute. They sang, yet to her surprise, she kept it together. Then Pastor Jim began the sermon, talking about the importance of fellowship, or doing life together. Dry-eyed, Kate proceeded to take detailed notes on the teaching for me. I brought my journal to church every week and took notes, both to better sink the lesson into my brain and so I'd have thoughts to refer back to. Knowing this about me, Kate correctly guessed I'd be jazzed to talk about Jesus and what she'd learned once she got back to the hospital, so she took notes.

Pastor Jim went on about how building a close-knit community is a core part of following Jesus and living a full life. As he wound down, he talked specifically concerning the value of small groups, particularly how they are instrumental in providing love, encouragement, and support in times of crisis. He then talked about my accident and the support Kate and my family had received from my small group, led by Dustin and Hope. With that, Kate's prophecy was fulfilled as buckets of tears began pouring from her eyes. Kate squeezed Leia's hand and let the mix of sorrow, joy, grief, and love wash over her. The release felt good; allowing herself to express what she was feeling was cleansing on a soul level.

I was sitting in my chair when Kate and Leia made it to the hospital. My nurse on that shift, Kathy, happened to be in the room at the time, so she gave them an update. "Lang's been rocking and rolling, trying to get himself out of the chair," she said. "Kate, I think you calm him down. Kermit, does Kate calm you down?"

"Yes," I nodded.

Kate smiled and said, "Lang calms me down too."

"You two are so cute and sweet together," my nurse observed with a grin as she wrapped up her duties.

I smiled at Kate throughout the conversation and eventually reached for her, until she placed her hand in my grasp. I gently held her hand with both of my hands while planting a few kisses on her lips. I cautiously and slowly brought her hand to my lips and started gently kissing it. I moved on to each finger in turn, savoring the moment with my fiancée. With these acts of touch and tenderness, time seemed to lose all meaning as our eyes met, and we sat looking at each other with broad, joy-filled smiles. An indeterminable amount of time later, Kate began to tear up. I pointed at her, expressing concern about her tears and not wanting her to be sad.

"I'm fine, Lang," she said. "I'm just so happy to be sharing this moment with you. Are you okay?"

"Yes," I nodded enthusiastically. I continued to hold her hand and began gently stroking it with my fingers.

That Sunday, a day shy of two weeks since the accident, was certainly one of the best days since my fall. The doctor spoke with Kate about my status and told her that as far as the hospital was concerned, I was ready for discharge from University Medical Center to inpatient rehabilitation elsewhere on Monday. Unfortunately, the air force still hadn't made a decision, but Kate expected words from them any day.

That night, Kevin Coyle, one of my friends from work, came by to see me and bring dinner for Leia and Kate. Basking in the afterglow of a good day and further steps forward in my recovery, they enjoyed the sweet-and-sour chicken, rice, Caesar salad, and pumpkin bread feast he'd brought for them.

One of the incredible things about love is its heavenly ability to transcend distances, differences, and even knowing someone directly. We were regularly amazed by how many encouraging and life-giving letters, cards, blog comments, and more I received from people all around the world, many of whom I'd never even met! For instance, as we sat enjoying a "good" day in the ICU, Leia and Kate shared with me how a lady in the air force had written to say that though she didn't know me personally, we'd both been at the same exercise conferences quite a few times. She'd noticed how kind and professional I was to everyone I interacted with, so when her unit commander told the troops about my accident and the blog Kate used to let people know how I was doing, she'd been reading it daily. With a word of blessing from across the country, this angel let us know we were in her and her husband's thoughts and prayers.

Eager to get us on to the next stage of recovery as soon as possible, Kate sought answers from the air force first thing on the morning of Monday, November 24. As they talked about the options for my rehabilitation, for the first time they mentioned they might not send me to Seattle, which was conveniently near our hometown. Instead, they were considering the VA hospital in Palo Alto, California, as a very real possibility. This was not what Kate, Leia, or I (even in my "unable to do anything about it" state) wanted to hear. The prospect of both having to leave the support of friends in Las Vegas and going to a place without family and a support system was quite sobering. Urged on by this unpleasant prospect, Kate quickly got in touch with the appropriate people to emphasize her and my family's view that I should go to Seattle for rehabilitation.

Greatly saddened by this turn of events, particularly the prospect of not being able to be near Leif, Kate prayed. "Lord, please hear my prayer. I am weak. I need you. I am sad. I need you. I am confused. I need you. Please hold me ... Please talk to me. Tell me you are here with us. I am scared. Please hold me, Lord … Thank you for saving Lang. Please continue to guide us on your path. I love you. In Jesus's name, amen."

Kate realized that although going to Palo Alto was not what she wanted, it might be part of God's plan, so she asked mainly for strength and comfort. Would the Lord answer?

As my two ladies entered the hospital, people began wishing Leia happy birthday. Guards, nurses, and doctors greeted her with the same wishes. Confusion crept across Leia's face until she finally asked Kate, "How did they know it was my birthday?"

Kate smiled and admitted that she had told them about the big day.

Pastor Doug visited later that afternoon, bearing gifts in the form of snacks for Kate and Leia. "Hi, Lang," he cheerfully called to me as he walked in. During this span of days, my being awake was the exception rather than the rule, but Pastor Doug was fortunate enough to come during one of my waking moments. In response to his greeting, I gave what Kate termed one of my "big Lang smiles," along with a thumbs-up. After getting caught up on Palo Alto being the next possible destination, Doug prayed for the situation and the sadness it was causing.

The pastor's visits made Kate feel closer to God and more connected, but they also reminded her of our relationship, which made her sad. As Doug left that day, Kate began crying while trying to hide it from me. I noticed, though, and concern became clear on my face. I pointed at her glossy eyes and trembling chin.

"I'm okay, Lang. I just really miss talking to you."

In response, I nodded yes and pointed at first myself and then to her. I then clearly mouthed, "I love you," which made Kate's tears pour all the faster. She leaned in and silently hugged me for a long moment as we comforted each other.

That evening, Kate and Leia's newfound community celebrated my sister's birthday. Karl and Alicia had them over for a celebratory dinner and cake, filling their bellies and brightening their spirits.

Later that night, Kate and I had another moment. I pointed to her, then to me, and finally to the door.

"Me and you go?" she asked.

I nodded an ardent yes.

"We are still waiting for approval from the military," Kate said with a sigh.

In response, I shrugged my shoulders and rolled my eyes, which gave Kate a good laugh.

A short while later, Leia came back to the room. I waved my hand at Kate a few times before she caught on that I was actually motioning for her to come closer. I tried to whisper in her ear, but I couldn't get any sound out.

"You can't talk," Kate explained to me.

I started trying to get my message across by doing charades with my hands. Kate guessed at what I meant several times, and I shook my head no at each. Determined to communicate, I then formed letters with my fingers to spell out my message in what would have been a fairly long process.

"Do I need to write this down?" Kate asked.

"Yes," I nodded with a smile, and out came Kate's journal and pen. She was planning to write out the letters I formed, but I had other ideas. I reached for the writing implements and began scribbling out barely legible phrases with my left hand. In my defense, I am right-handed (which was broken). I managed to get out several lines before my writing grew too sloppy to read, and I threw the pen in frustration.

Here's the partially sensible and applicable fragments I was able to communicate.

"Do I need to practice anything? Like pre football practice?"
"Make nurse play before exercises?"
"Being victim?"
"Being rescued?"
"Talk about health care today?"

It didn't all make sense, but within the context of the day's events, it seemed I was aware enough about the transfer issue and Kate and Leia's frustrations, and I, too, was concerned. In addition, I was trying to better understand my current physical condition so I could improve it.

Kate and Leia's arrival on the twenty-fifth began with them bursting into laughter upon looking at me. In their continuing efforts to try to prevent me from yanking out my tubes or get out of bed, the nurses had put new contraptions on my arms; Kate called them "sandbag arm floaties." What looked like the floaties kids wear in the pool when they're little and can't swim well, were filled with sand and strapped to each of my arms. They were so heavy that I couldn't bend my arms, move them quickly, or even move them very much at all. When Leia and Kate first saw me, I lay asleep with my floaties on, arms up over my head, feet touching, and knees bent out to the sides. In other words, the ladies started howling in laughter because I looked like a frog, which was especially apropos for someone nicknamed Kermit.

A little while later, the nurse came in and shared news that made the scene not as funny. She told them why I had the floaties on instead of the mitts I'd previously worn. Even with the mitts on, I had ripped my feeding tube from my belly. The doctors couldn't simply put a new one back in because the hole had closed up, so a new tube would require another surgery. That said, they agreed it was important to limit the number of surgeries I had, so they determined it was best to wait until my mouth was ready to be unwired shut and do both surgeries at once.

Not long after the ladies got caught up on my latest adventures, their less-than-wonderful results, and the plan to fix me up, I woke up. I did some more writing with Kate, this time indicating that I didn't know where we were.

"Do you want me to tell you about where we are?" Kate asked.
"Yes."

Kate began telling me we were in Las Vegas, at the trauma center because of an accident, and we had been there for two weeks.

I shrugged and lay back in my chair, indicating I understood.

Unsure about how much I really remembered, Kate asked me if I remembered the accident and why I was in the hospital.

"No," I shook my head.

Kate and Leia recounted the story of my terrible fall and the miraculous healing of God in saving my life. This same conversation began occurring on a daily basis. I couldn't remember the accident, which was understandable, but what became disturbing was that I couldn't recall that Kate had told me about it on a previous day. This was perhaps the first sign that my recovery was going to take a turn for the worse.

Still, on November 25, I was doing incredibly well for having fallen thirty feet off a cliff onto rocks headfirst. Many friends and family attributed, and continue to do so, the speed and extent of my recovery to family and friends being a loving, hope-filled presence every step of the way.

That day, Kevin told my fiancée, "Kate, words cannot express how thankful I am for all that you are doing for our friend Lang. You are saving his life every day!"

While Kate was my most frequent and constant companion in the hospital, our connection and her expressions of love for and toward me were small pieces of a greater communal love puzzle. Many people in the hospital noticed how I had a constant stream of friends and family coming to visit and care for me. Like moths drawn to a flame, employees would regularly join my people, either in my room or the waiting room, to drink from the flow of love we had between us. Whether they simply checked on me when they didn't really need to, made small talk, or opened up and shared about their lives, over and over again, hospital workers came to join the tangible giving and receiving of love via attention, care, and kindness that flowed between my family, friends, and me.

Love isn't only contagious and attractive, though—it's also expansive. Our story of loving-kindness spread in the hands of friends and family to touch and inspire many others. Exuding the joy of someone plotting a big surprise birthday party, Dustin, my Bible study group leader, shared how he'd witnessed firsthand the potent impact of my story and the healing love of my family and friends. He taught CPR, and while we faced the painful ups, downs, and process of my recovery, in two weeks of classes, he'd shared the tale with 150 people to remind them tomorrow is not guaranteed, so let's live each minute to the fullest. (In July 2010, he estimated the total had increased to five thousand.) We're here to share God's love with one another, he told us, and we've been a beautiful example of this to others. As Paul wrote in Romans with awe and gratitude, Dustin concluded, God was busy turning a tragic accident into a positive situation, "And we know that God causes all things to work together for good to those who love God, to those who are called according to His purposes" (Romans 8:28 New American Standard Bible).

Enlivened by the light of Dustin, Kevin, and others, late that night, I once again felt like "chatting," so I gestured for some pen and paper. With my brow furrowed in concentration, I wrote another round of questions, neater this time.

"How are the Seahawks doing?" I asked. I am a die-hard fan of all Seattle sports teams, and even with a traumatic brain injury, I was still rooting for my home team.

Then came a less lighthearted question. I was worried about the welfare of my fiancée and sister and so asked, "What are you doing for work?"

Leia plunged in with an answer while Kate remained silent. Leia told me, "I am on extended paid leave, so don't worry brother."

Not letting Kate get away with not telling her tale, I turned and pointed to her. She smiled and looked the other direction before talking to me about her status. "As of yesterday, I am officially unemployed. Because we aren't married, I could not qualify for extended paid leave."

My eyes bulged in surprise like saucers.

"You're supporting me now," Kate said while smiling at me, which made my eyes grow even bigger. Kate laughed and continued.

"We have everything under control. You're my new job now, so I want a raise."

I gave her a half smile of amusement and satisfaction and shrugged my shoulders. "What are we paying for?" I added.

"Are you worried about our budget?" Kate queried.

I nodded, a diligent planner at heart.

"We have everything under control," Kate replied in a soothing voice. "Don't worry about it." In fact, Leia was in charge of my finances. She oversaw my bank and credit card accounts, made sure all my bills were paid, ensured Lara's mom received child support, and even tithed for me to VBF every month. She was so thorough that even my United Airlines frequent flyer account address was changed to her house.

In retrospect, it blows my mind how loving and caring Leia was during this time. She had two young boys then (now three), and both she and her husband (Erick) worked full-time. Still, they figured out a way for her to stay and care for me for several weeks. And as if that wasn't enough, on top of keeping track of her family's finances, she did mine. Wow!

Happy the ladies were taken care of, I wondered, "What do the doctors say about how I'm doing?"

Kate recounted all my injuries and the current plan for getting me back to full health. I put my hands together in a gesture of prayer and shook them forward and back.

"Are you saying, 'Thank God'?" Kate said.

"Yes," I indicated, expressing amazement at our Creator and Sustainer's healing power.

To conclude the evening, Kate broke out some pictures of Lara to show me, telling me how she had moved back to Washington with her mom as planned. I smiled from ear to ear at the thought of my little girl, beaming the way only a proud parent could. Then tears began gathering in my eyes until they spilled over my lashes. I hadn't seen Lara in two weeks and wouldn't until mid-February.

Frequently, within the span of minutes, Kate, Leia, others, and

I went from laughter to tears and vice versa. We felt our joy, sorrow, frustration, hope, and everything else. There's something magical about both being fully in tune with one's inner landscape, and being able to vulnerably share your inside reality with others. It seems to me the combination of feeling and healthily expressing all our feels is vital to experiencing the abundant life Jesus desires to give us. What is more, we don't have to be happy or sad, peaceful or angry, thankful or troubled; we can be both simultaneously. That's why in the story of my accident (a tragic event) there are both moments of consolation and desolation, rejoicing and heartache.

To walk through this crazy adventure we call life together, while loving each other well through it, requires us to communally weep and laugh, rejoice and mourn, shout for gladness and howl in anger, and so on. To achieve this means we must be present both to others and to our own raw and authentic selves, which means as much as possible putting aside concerns about the past and worries over the future in order to be fully rooted in the here and now. From this vantage point, we can decipher and effectively process what's going on in our own soul. This awareness is what allowed Kate to cry for the losses and pain, laugh and make fun of my feeble antics, and tear up for the joy of an intimate embrace. Further, this presence in the here and now is also what enables us to be aware and curious of what's going on with others, which is a powerful gift. Although she doesn't come up in this story as much as Kate or me, Leia was a conscious and connected presence who played an invaluable role in freeing and empowering us to feel and express the diverse emotions the accident, recovery, and its repercussions brought up. In other words, Leia was a safe space for people to be fully alive and fully human in all its messiness. I pray you have truly safe and nonjudgmental friends like Leia, with whom you can let your emotional, spiritual, and relational hair down, so to speak, because it is a wonderful gift.

This brings to mind Pixar's film *Inside Out*. The animated flick hilariously depicts the emotions inside a young lady's head as individual characters. Joy, Sadness, Fear, Anger, and Disgust are each personified, with only one being able to take control of the girl's actions at a time. Early on, the emotions come to an unspoken yet explicit agreement that Joy is the best emotion and Sadness is the worst. They spend much of the movie attempting to keep Joy in the driver's seat and Sadness out. The problem with this is we are wonderfully complex creatures who are meant to feel and healthily express our full spectrum of emotions. As you can imagine, the repression of Sadness leads to all sorts of unhealthiness, chaos, and emotional explosions. In my mind, *Inside Out*'s characters would have done well to learn from the ways my family and my friends were present, vulnerable, and supportive enough to healthily feel and process their full spectrum of emotions. In short, that's part of what it means to be fully human and fully alive.

We see this frequently in the Bible's book of Psalms. The Psalms are songs, poems, or prayers, which are widely considered words of worship to God. Interestingly, however, the largest class of psalms is the lament. Of the 150 psalms, more than 40 percent center on complaints, worries, fears, anguishes, and protests to the Creator. When people or the events of life led the Psalms' authors to feeling what are generally considered "negative" emotions, like anger, frustration, fear, sadness, and despair, instead of bottling them up, they poetically and worshipfully expressed them to God.

After all, isn't our Creator, whom we call Father, the safest being in the universe to be and express our complete selves to? Isn't that part of what God desires by passionately seeking relationship with us? The writers of the Psalms think so, expressing themselves in such raw and unfiltered ways that even the director of the goriest of movies today would cringe. For instance, consider the following.

> Happy shall they be who take your little ones and dash them against the rock! (Psalm 137:9 New Revised Standard Version)

> O God, break the teeth in their mouths. (Psalm 58:6a New Revised Standard Version)

> The righteous will rejoice when they see vengeance done; they will bathe their feet in the blood of the wicked. (Psalm 28:10 New Revised Standard Version)

> Let burning coals fall on them! Let them be flung into pits, no more to rise! (Psalm 140:10 New Revised Standard Version)

Having myself ranted, raged, and cursed in my journal when I felt really hurt by someone, I don't think the writers wanted these terrors to occur. I say that because I didn't really think the strong words I used to describe people, when I vented, were truthful characterizations of them, or that they deserved the torment I wished upon them. Instead, what I'm saying, and I think the psalmists were expressing, is that frustrations and hurts are like boiling water trapped in a sealed container: you have to let out the steam, or else the pressure will build and you'll blow.

To put it differently, when we don't express, vent, and let out our angers, despairs, and frustrations, they will warp and twist us from the inside out. I think bottling up and suppressing our feelings is a recipe for addiction, depression, insecurities, infidelity, and worse. In my mind, that's a major reason why the Psalms contain numerous prayers asking God to do terrible things to other people. If we don't get our feelings out in healthy ways, like prayers, safe conversations, and journals, then they will inevitably manifest themselves in harmful words or deeds. This is one reason why I include Kate's laments to God in this story: because to be fully alive is to be fully honest with God, each other (in a life-giving manner), and yourself.

9

The Setback

Jesus asked the father, "How long has this been happening to him?" And he said, "From childhood. It has often cast him into the fire and into the water, to destroy him; but if you are able to do anything, have pity on us and help us." Jesus said to him, "If you are able! — All things can be done for the one who believes." Immediately the father of the child cried out, "I believe; help my unbelief!" (Mark 9:21–24 The Message)

The day before Thanksgiving, Kate walked in to see me sitting up in bed and gazing toward the door. "Good morning, sunshine," she cheerfully called.

"Good morning," I said in a full-volume, close to normal, but slightly Kermitlike voice.

Kate's mouth hung open for an instant before she ran to my side, hugging me and squealing in joy. My newfound voice was the result of the doctors capping my trach and giving me a valve, which allowed me to talk.

When Kate's affections subsided, I cleared my voice. "I have been waiting for you for three hours."

With a soft chuckle in response to my lonely lover look, Kate reminded me, "Visiting hours don't start until 9:00 a.m., dear."

Nodding in understanding, I asked where the kids were.

"In Washington with their other parents," she reassured me.

"Oh, I thought you would have them with you," I answered.

"Leif is coming soon though," she quickly added, "and I'll bring him in to see you."

"Leif is still eight years old, right?" I queried.

Laughing, Kate replied, "Yes, we haven't been here for *that* long."

Isn't it amazing how we take little things for granted? Like the ability to talk? Because I hadn't been able to speak for a while and limited in my communication, this particular morning was a joyful verbal reunion of sorts.

As we rejoiced over this new reality, Pam walked into the room. Kate greeted her, smiled, and introduced me by explaining, "Pam's the one who has been taking care of me."

"Thank you," I said, my eyes shining with gratitude.

Kate turned to the social worker and asked her to get Leia. "But don't tell her Lang can talk," she added conspiratorially.

As my sister walked in, I said, "Hi!"

With a huge grin, Leia quickly glided over and gave me a delighted bear hug.

Seizing upon my newfound ability to express myself, a virtual torrent of questions poured out of my mouth. "Can you get me some food?" "Can we leave?" "Why can't we leave?" and "What are we waiting for?" were among my areas of interest.

The staff did eventually bring me some food, which I was able to eat on my own. By *eat* I mean I managed to get at least a small portion of the food into my mouth. Much of the soup, pudding, milk, and lemonade ended up on my hands and face. Still, the small fact that I was feeding myself was cause for celebration in Kate's and Leia's eyes.

Finally, later that day the physical therapists got me out of bed and walking down the hall. Kate strolled alongside me, holding my arm and beaming like she did on our first date. When I had previously "walked" in the hospital it had actually been more of a shuffling of my feet. This day I walked with purpose, taking normal steps down the hall.

Falling Into Love

"Slow down, Lang," the therapists said. No kidding, they actually had to tell me to slow down.

Leif flew in to visit for Thanksgiving, joining Leia and Kate to stay at my friend Julie's house. On the morning of Turkey Day, the three arrived at the hospital just as visiting hours commenced. Kate went back to the room and found me talking to Josh, noticing I was holding myself more upright than usual. As she thought about this, though, she realized I always held myself straighter and more erect when air force friends were at the hospital. It was as if at a subconscious level, I considered their visits somehow akin to being at work again.

"Do you want to see Leif?" Kate asked me.

"Yes, please."

Josh went to get him while she stayed in the room and talked to me. "Did you eat breakfast?" she asked.

Groggily and a bit zoned out, I slowly answered, "I don't know. I can't remember."

When Leif came in, I quickly held my arms out to bring him in for a hug. I followed up with a fist bump because that was how we rolled.

After the initial excitement of our greeting had subsided, Leif sat quietly, taking in all the tubes and machines hooked to me with a pensive look on his face. Noticing his hesitancy, Kate set about easing his discomfort by explaining to him what each item in the room did for me.

This naturally prompted Leif to ask a typical boy question. "How does he go to the bathroom?"

Kate explained that I couldn't get up to use the bathroom, so the hospital staff attached a tube to my privates to take away all the pee. "It's called a catheter," she said.

Listening in, I turned toward Leia and remarked, "She did a good job explaining all that."

As usual, around lunchtime Kate left with Leia, and now Leif too, during a break in visiting hours. Yet much like how weather can abruptly shift from sunny to stormy, in that small chunk of time, my condition veered dramatically. When she returned a few hours later, she arrived in the room to see me staring off into space, fixated on nothing.

"Is everything okay?" my fiancée voiced with a hint of concern in her voice.

I turned my head in her direction, looking toward her but not at her. I didn't say anything.

With an elevating amount of worry creeping into her voice, Kate said, "Can you answer a few questions?"

"Yes." This time I gave a response.

"What's the last thing you remember before being in the hospital?" she wondered, trying to gauge my mental state.

"Taking care of my sister … I think." Something I hadn't done since high school, over fifteen years prior to these events.

Continuing to keep it simple, she probed further by asking, "When is your birthday?"

I moved my hands and fingers around, attempting to make some sort of gesture. It was unintelligible to Kate, and I said nothing.

"What's your middle name?" she continued.

"Matthew," I answered correctly.

I hadn't said her name at all since she'd returned, so Kate breathed deeply, swallowed, and asked, "What is my name?"

I mumbled something.

"I couldn't hear you. Can you repeat that?"

Again I made an unclear sound.

"Lang, do you know what my name is?" Kate wondered.

"Tell me," came my heart-ripping response.

"Do you need me to tell you because you can't remember?"

"Yes," I said, still staring blankly.

With tears building she said, "Kate."

"Keep going," I replied.

"Kate Walton," she answered as she struggled to dam the flood of tears ready to spill down her face. "Do you remember the name of the little boy who was in to see you earlier?"

I shook my head. "No."

"Leif," she said.

I repeated, "Kate Walton and Leif," as if I were trying the names on my lips for the first time.

Unable to fight back her emotions any longer, Kate rose quickly and kissed my cheek. "I'm going to get your sister," she sobbed as she fled the room.

I just sat there, eyes empty, body still, and with no verbal response.

As Kate entered the waiting room, Leia noticed the look on her faced and knew something was amiss. "What's wrong, Kate?"

Kate recounted my blank expression and the conversation with me, expressing she was very worried I'd forget her altogether because we'd been dating only a matter of months. Exacerbating this fear was that one of Kate's cousins, whom she is close to, had suffered a somewhat similar traumatic brain injury years before, and she had permanently lost months of her memory from before her accident.

Giving Kate a comforting embrace, Leia assured her, "He knows who you are. There's going to be days like this." After a few moments, she went back to my room to see me herself.

There I sat, looking distantly at nothing in particular, not noticing my sister. "Hey, brother, do you remember my name?" Leia asked.

"No." I didn't even remember my own sister's name.

Leia talked to my nurse and explained what had transpired. She told Leia, "Kermit's going to have good days and bad days. This is just a bad day." Hoping to ease some of my fiancée's pain, Leia relayed this information to Kate. Although the "bad day" notion made intellectual sense, it made no sense to her heart. What was more, Kate had the gut feeling that something worse was going on than a bad day.

Amid this feeling of unrest, as people are often apt to do,

that night the ladies and Leif found some comfort in food. It was Thanksgiving, and Julie prepared a wonderful spread for them. The main fair was delightful, and her turkey, though done, was still moist enough to drip juices as it melted in their mouths, covered with a celebratory portion of gravy. What was more, Julie provided them with other typical holiday staples like mashed potatoes, stuffing, green bean casserole, pumpkin pie, and apple pie. Wine completed the meal, adding a festive air to the occasion. Julie's excellent cooking and friendly hospitality made everything seem a little less dreary to my crew after the feast.

After dinner, they returned to the hospital, hoping and praying for a positive sign. I sat asleep in my chair, slumping forward and drooling. Kate attempted to get me to wake up while rearranging me into a more comfortable position. I did come out of my slumber, but I remained totally unresponsive with the same dull, lifeless stare.

Jeffrey, one of the talented ICU nurses, came in. "Kermit will probably be up rocking and rolling tonight after you leave. It's what he usually does," he said in an effort to soothe Leia and Kate's anxiety.

Wondering whether my medication had anything to do with my change in behavior, Kate asked if there had been any changes. Jeffrey assured her that they were still the same. As he was pointing this out, I looked at Kate and stretched for her with my hand. Sitting in front of me, she leaned into my embrace. For a moment, I actually looked at her and smiled. Then it was gone, and I was back to being conscious but not present. Still, she was incredibly thankful for that brief minute.

Kate cried quite a bit on Thanksgiving. At a soul level, my conscious unconsciousness and not being able to remember her name was more traumatic than the initial accident was. Still, it's quite possible she became even sadder the next day.

Although physically I showed some signs of improvement by going for a walk, sitting in the chair, and eagerly shoving chocolate

Falling Into Love

pudding into my mouth, I was still largely unresponsive, and when I tried to talk, all that came out was incoherent mumbling.

To make matters worse, Leia and Leif left that day. For the first time since the accident, Kate was without family. She was far from home and now without Leia, Leif, and the rest, deep down she felt intensely alone. What was more, during Leif's two-day visit, she could see in his expressions how much he missed her and how much he needed his mom to be around. She felt so deeply the need to take care of her boy that Kate began thinking of going home to him for a short time while having my mom come to watch me. Face and hands damp from tears, on Black Friday she whispered to me in a cracked voice, "My heart is completely broken right now."

On Saturday, November 29, my nurse tried to wake me up to no avail. She pinched and jiggled me, but I kept sleeping. Coming on the heels of my two "bad days," this troubled her and got the staff's attention. When I finally did wake up, it was with a fit of mucus-filled coughing. I could barely breathe, with all the liquid buildup in my throat and lungs.

In response, the doctor ordered a CAT scan on my head as soon as possible. He told Kate they were concerned I had bleeding in my brain. The threat this turn of events was going to give me brain damage was real, and Kate fearfully let as many friends and family know about this dire situation as possible, asking for prayers the doctors would be able to quickly diagnose my condition and fix it before my brain was permanently damaged.

In response to Kate's plea, my angel, Julie, offered her prayers and the following encouraging quote from Edward Teller: "When you come to the end of all the light you know, and it's time to step into the darkness of the unknown, faith is knowing that one of two things shall happen: Either you will be given something solid to stand on or you will be taught to fly."

Finding herself at her end, Kate cried out to Jesus. She prayed, "Dear Lord, Lang has left me. I haven't seen him in two days. When I look into his eyes, I don't see him. I see an empty shell. He isn't fighting anymore. Please, Lord, could you reach down and heal him? I know you saved his life, but I fear that he is slipping away."

After examining the CAT scan, the neurosurgeon met with Kate. "There's no bleeding in the brain, which is good. However, there is extra brain fluid floating around. The condition is not an emergency, so we'll evaluate Lang in the morning."

Sunday morning, Kate walked in to a sight she'd hoped to never see again: me lying in bed with a bolt in my head once more. Dr. Smith, the neurosurgeon, had decided earlier that it was a necessary step because not only was my excess brain fluid causing my nonresponsiveness, it had also begun causing me to have seizures. The bolt was meant to monitor the pressure in my head and drain any excess brain fluid. Loaded up with antiseizure medicine, I laid there comatose as Dr. Smith filled Kate in on the most current situation.

Dr. O spoke to Kate after lunch with more words about my current condition. He explained, "We put Lang's central line back in to feed him via his IV. If he's unable to feed himself in a few days, I'll have to surgically insert a stronger, thicker tube into his stomach. This would be a major surgery because it would require me to cut open his stomach." Sighing, he added, "I know you were hoping to go to Seattle soon, Kate, but unfortunately you're going to be here at least one more week … if all goes well. Also, so that you're prepared, we think it's possible he'll have some brain damage from the seizures he's having. Though he might not." If this were a movie, I'm sure ominous music would have accompanied Dr. O's closing remarks.

I got another CAT scan later that day, this one bearing more bad news. There was no change in my status, which meant the bolt wasn't draining my brain fluid or it wasn't in correctly.

Worn out by several incredibly emotional days, that evening Kate sat by my side … alone. A young black man, the janitor, walked in and smiled at Kate, as he had nearly every day she'd been in the hospital.

"What's your name?" he asked.

Falling Into Love

"Kate. How about you?" she replied.

"Stacy, spelled the boy's way, without the *E*," he answered. He looked over at the board in my room covered with pictures and scriptures filled with hope, pointed at the Bible verses, and said in a strong and firm voice, "I believe that."

Believing God was up to something through this young man, Kate nodded. "I do too, and so does Lang."

Grinning at Kate like a boy about to reveal a good secret, Stacy added, "The doctors aren't the ones who heal people. It's God and prayer. I've been praying for Lang. Don't always listen to what the doctors say because they usually make it sound worse than it actually is."

Eyes glistening, Kate thanked Stacy. "I appreciate that."

After gathering the garbage, Stacy paused for a quick story. "Kermit scared me one night, you know. I was cleaning up his room, and all of a sudden, he moved to his side. I thought he was getting out of bed." Laughing to himself, Stacy continued. "I almost ran out of the room until I looked over, and Kermit was giving me a thumbs-up."

Kate got a good chuckle out of Stacy's adventure.

Before leaving the room, he concluded by saying, "I can tell Kermit is going to get better. He has a good spirit."

A while later, I came to for a short time, right before Kate left to eat. I looked directly at my fiancée with real warmth in my eyes, not the cold and distant look of previous days.

Holding my hand, Kate wondered, "Can you squeeze my hand, Lang?"

My pinkie wiggled a little.

"I felt the pinkie. Could you try again?" she said to encourage me.

Understanding what Kate was after, I put all my effort into it and gave her a very weak squeeze of the hand. The nurse happened to notice the exchange and further lifted Kate's spirits by saying, "Now, that is purposeful! That's a good sign." The ICU staff was trained to look for a patient to respond to commands in a deliberate manner to help judge mental health and wellness.

For the next twenty minutes, Kate sat there talking to me, telling me about the brain fluid and other troubles. "You're so strong, honey," she continued. "Keep praying and keep fighting." She went on to describe how I'd touched so many people without even knowing it. "You'd be proud of the outpouring of love, mercy, and grace from your friends and family. Not only can you feel it, you can see it."

As she began to go into how our family now appreciated time together in a way they never had before, and she described the effects of these events on others, I reached up with both my hands and turned my body toward her. Gripping my hands, Kate looked softly into my eyes. I began weakly tugging on her arms, trying to pull her toward me while craning my neck toward her.

"If you're asking for a kiss, give me a thumbs-up, dear." Kate said with a smile.

The fastest thumbs-up she's probably ever seen in her life ensued. She then planted a long kiss on me with her soft, full lips.

"You definitely deserved that one," she added.

Not long later, while Kate was still glowing from our moment, I began convulsing with a seizure. My left arm began shaking uncontrollably. A few moments later, my head followed suit. All Kate could do was talk to me with a calm and soothing voice while holding my hand until the tremors eventually subsided.

December 1 saw the neurologist come in to perform an EEG, a procedure used to determine how well my brain synapses were firing. Specifically, this test of my brain's electrical activity would help the staff learn more about my uncontrollable shaking and trembling. The neurologist attached a plethora of wires to my head to perform the scan, making me look like a character in some futuristic movie about an advanced civilization.

"Everything looks normal," he reported. "I don't think he'll have any more seizures. I'm fairly certain the excess fluid caused them, and because that's being treated, they should go away."

Later, Dr. Smith looked me over and gave Kate more sobering news. "We will be putting in a shunt to assist his body in draining the excess brain fluid. This is a permanent thing, but it's completely livable and common with head injuries." A shunt is a long tube, controlled by a programmable chip, that drains the excess cerebrospinal fluid from the brain down into the abdominal cavity. Because it has a computer chip, exposure to large magnets scramble the programming, which causes the shunt to malfunction, meaning a person with a shunt shouldn't have MRIs or go through metal detectors.

"The bolt will stay until he can breathe without the assistance of pressure. Lang is really sick and still in a life-threatening condition. I'm still confident that he will make a full recovery. That said, I want to warn you that he has a good six to twelve months of recovery ahead of him," Dr. Smith concluded.

In short, three weeks after my accident, Dr. Smith both thought my life was still at risk and was confident I was going to fully recover. Further, although my excess brain fluid had caused a significant and traumatic setback in my recovery, Kate both believed God was going to help everything turn out well and was scared it wouldn't.

I think they were giving voice to the same thing the father at the beginning of the chapter hinted at by beseeching Jesus with, "I believe; help my unbelief"—namely nondual thinking. Nondual thinking is being able to hold together notions we usually consider as opposites (i.e., belief and unbelief), though its sister, dualistic thinking, is largely the default in the West. Whereas nondual thinking approaches things from a "both/and" perspective, dualism sees everything in terms of "either/or." The first way, for instance, gives space for the father to both believe and not believe, whereas the second attitude would insist he must be either one or the other.

Now, don't get me wrong. A dualistic stance definitely has its time and place. It helps us drive, shop, cook, clean, respond to threats, make quick decisions, and so on. The problem comes when we let dualistic thinking define our realities. By doing so, we set people, things, and ideas in opposition to each other. When we approach things from an either/or mentality, there's a quick and slippery slope to division, adversity, and conflict. The side we prefer or pick is naturally "right" or "good" in our eyes, which makes the other side "wrong" or "bad." Thus, Republican or Democrat easily becomes Republican versus Democrat, theist (one who believes in God) or atheist naturally turns into theist versus atheist, gay or straight transforms into gay versus straight, black or white falls into black versus white, and so on.

Dualistic thinking leaves no in-between. Although this is helpful for driving a car or buying groceries, quite frankly, life isn't a black or white affair; it's more of a messy pallet full of all the colors. Dualistic, either/or thinking leaves people, races, and countries divided and opposed to each other. It fails to take a holistic approach, which recognizes Republicans and Democrats both make good points and stand for good things. Dualism refuses to accept Middle Eastern peoples and terrorist have every right to be upset at the United States for putting military bases in their countries, and/or conducting military operations in their lands, and/or overtly or covertly manipulating their government, and/or using economic sanctions and the like to impose our will on their nations. Simultaneously, US citizens have every right to be upset by terrorist acts and respond to them.

More to the point, dualistic thinking fails to wrap its mind around big, messy, and/or paradoxical topics and experiences like God, faith, death, trauma, forgiveness, and love. Love knows no bounds. It's able to include opposites. It was able to believe I would be okay while simultaneously realizing I could still die.

Love seeks to unite and bring sides together, rather than divide or harm. It recognizes belief and unbelief can coexist, faith and doubt belong together, one God is multiple persons, and so on. It sees no side or person as better than the other. Everyone is in the image of God and worthy of kindness, care, and compassion because there really is no separation between any of us; we are truly one humanity, one family under God. Everything and everyone belong.

Nondual thinking levels the playing field. It is the mindset of grace, the realization we never did and never will have to do anything to earn love or salvation. Instead, they are free gifts offered to us because we have always been and always will be children of our Creator.

10

Vampire Love

Just then a religion scholar stood up with a question to test Jesus. "Teacher, what do I need to do to get eternal life?"

He answered, "What's written in God's Law? How do you interpret it?"

He said, "That you love the Lord your God with all your passion and prayer and muscle and intelligence—and that you love your neighbor as well as you do yourself."

"Good answer!" said Jesus. "Do it and you'll live."
(Luke 10:25–28, The Message)

With my Thanksgiving setback diagnosed and treated, December saw me once again on the upswing. An early December Monday found me awake a large portion of the day for a change, frequently holding Kate's hand, and giving everyone who passed by a thumbs-up. I even felt perky enough to watch the Monday Night Football game. It wasn't the Seahawks or even a good game, but by all indications I enjoyed it. Still, our pleasurable evening was periodically interrupted by fits of coughing up dark, thick mucus—a troublesome sign I was developing pneumonia.

Less than a month since the accident, cards, letters, gift cards, and well-wishes on the blog continued to regularly flood my room and the hearts of my family, friends, and me. That day I received a card from a boy's Scout troop, who was the son of the sister of one of my friends from work (say that three times fast!). Kate was nearly always there with me, but friends and family from elsewhere frequently flew in to stay and sit with me in love, and my local air force and church friends were regularly faces of transformative healing at my side. The massive outpouring of love via cards, gifts, prayers, calls, and comments on the blog was life-giving and amazing beyond words. Truly, their love coupled with the tangible, caring kindness of people physically present combined with the ineffable strength of God to save and carry not only me but Kate, my family, and my friends. I am eternally grateful!

Ali and Martha arrived from Tucson the next day to give Kate some much-needed company for a week. Ali, a tall, thin woman with long brown hair and a warm and friendly face, is Matt's wife. I'd met her, Matt, Martha, Danny, and other great friends through a church small group in Tucson. She has this laugh that bursts out from the depths of her lungs, ringing out loudly enough to practically be heard in a nearby town. It's not an "ouch, that hurts my ears" volume; it's a laugh that when you hear it, you can't help but smile and join her.

Martha is Danny's wife. She is the kind of lady who doesn't have a mean bone in her body; sweetness, loving, and caring are the fabric of her being. More than once, she's told me something to the effect of, "I felt very protective of you in the hospital," in a maternal, warm, and caring kind of way. Not only did their arrival bring good cheer to me, but they received the gift of the most encouraging medical news in some time when the doctor told them the fluid was now draining properly from my brain.

With that under control, it seemed I was back on the path to recovery, which enabled me to be largely awake, aware, and interactive for a second day in a row. Taking advantage of this opportunity, Kate read one of my favorite books to me, *Sex God* by Rob Bell. It paints a picture of how spirituality, sex, relationships, and God are all related and interconnected. In my mind, it beautifully illustrates

Falling Into Love

how we humans are loving, relational creatures made in the image of a loving and relational deity. Sex, then, is nothing less than a human-to-human experience of a relationship so intimate and loving it's a tangible picture of heaven come to earth. It's a mirror of the closeness God desires with each of us.

While Kate read the book, I lay in bed focusing on every word, absorbing it all. Whenever she tried to stop reading, I reached over and touched her, my silent way of saying, "Keep going."

In the morning, one of my brothers in the military visited me as soon as visiting hours began. Paul, whose call sign was Java, was a pilot for the EA-6B, a navy jet with a purpose very similar to my aircraft's. Java was an instructor at the navy's equivalent of the Weapons School. We knew each other from Weapons School exercises and various conferences, but also because he'd married one of my mentors from my early days flying as a crewmember on the EC-130H (Kathy, call sign Trixie). He was stationed on Whidbey Island, Washington, not too far from my hometown. Whenever possible, I tried to arrange work trips there, and I had been invited over to their place for dinner more than once.

Java talked about the current exercise, December's version of the Mission Employment event I described at the beginning of the book. He also told me how Trixie and his kid were doing. I was totally engaged in his stories about the exercise and family life, so much so that I repeatedly leaned toward him and animatedly moved my arms up and down as he talked. I tend to talk with my hands, so my "Langness" was really shining through that morning.

After Java left and before Kate arrived, I went into a seizure. As the doctors were making their rounds, my arms and head began convulsing uncontrollably. As troubling as this may sound, it wasn't anything abnormal. I'd been regularly shaking in this manner; think of it as a small-scale, nontroubling (to professionals) seizure, like one in a series of normal aftershocks to my brain trauma from the accident. My point is this episode, although freaky looking to the untrained eye, almost certainly didn't require any additional medication or treatment, but the physicians on hand weren't familiar with my tremors. Deciding this spasm was an emergency and needed attention, the doctor gave me a large amount of Ativan, a potent drug used to treat epilepsy. The drug knocked me out for the vast majority of the day.

When Kate, Ali, and Martha arrived that morning, Dr. Floyd, the resident, met them and gave them the bad news. "Kermit had a seizure, so we had to give him Ativan, a powerful sedative."

Ironically, as I lay passed out, Kate finally heard from the air force that day concerning my transition from the ICU and move to inpatient rehab. They wanted me to depart for the center as soon as possible. A short time ago, that would have been exciting and meant tomorrow, but after the brain fluid episode, the staff was again in the process of getting me medically stable, and when combined with that morning's seizure, meant leaving was still a week or two in the future. Furthermore, instead of essentially going home to Seattle, the air force decided I should go to the VA hospital in Palo Alto, California, because they specialized in brain trauma.

Although it was neither the location we longed for nor the best of days to receive the news, it did represent a positive step. Even though the Thanksgiving episode had set back me and everyone else, and I wasn't quite as recovered as I'd been beforehand, I was doing well again. The seizures I was experiencing weren't troubling and were part and parcel to severe TBI, meaning aside from my somewhat worrisome cough, I was improving across the board. That said, my seizures being "normal" illustrates how abnormal this whole experience was, and even with reassurances from the medical professionals about them, I imagine my spasms were always troubling to family, friends, and I.

By early December, I was making considerable progress. I was regularly conscious, present, andal interactive with guests. Now that we had a game plan from the air force for my next step, Kate and I decided to speed up the process by consistently doing some physical therapy exercises while she visited me.

Having almost entirely done nothing but lie in bed for nearly a month, the medical staff said I needed to work on my mobility, motor skills, and strength. What's more, the combination of inactivity and getting fed only through the IV was causing my weight to drop quickly. I was pretty skinny before the accident, at six feet tall and about 150 pounds, so after having already lost a good bit of weight, I was starting to look rail thin—a bit like Skeletor from *He-Man*, if you remember the cartoon. An air force friend of mine, Jon Rhone, had the following to say about the situation: "I must say, as skinny as Kermit is, the last thing he needs is for his jaw to be wired shut and rely on an IV for all his nutrients."

With all of this in mind, Kate and I passed some of the time by doing simple physical therapy exercises. Channeling her inner bank branch manager, she'd say, "Lift your right leg please, Lang," and I'd move in response. This was followed by left leg lifts, arm lifts, feet circles, and finger flexes.

Now that I was once more stable and improving, the staff decided they could again remove the bolt from my head and put a shunt in as the permanent solution for draining my brain fluid. They scheduled the surgery for 2:00 p.m. on an early December afternoon. Ali and Martha seized this opportunity to spirit away Kate from the hospital to relieve some stress and have some fun.

They went and saw *Twilight*, the first in a series of movies based on the books about romance, love, vampires, and werewolves. This tale, based on a young adult book series, was a phenomenon sweeping the nation at the time. After enjoying the film, Kate called and discovered although it was after two, I hadn't gone into surgery yet. Off they went to Julie's house for supper, with the assurance I'd be out of the operating room and ready for company when visiting hours resumed. They returned at 8:00 p.m.

When Kate walked up to the guard station at 8:04 to sign in and get her badge, the security guard called out, "There you are! Where have you been?"

"I know! I'm four minutes late! It's completely unacceptable," came Kate's playful response.

A smile split his face as he replied, "Four minutes is four minutes."

Chuckling, Kate finished with, "Four minutes I will never get back. I know."

Kate walked toward my room with excitement and anticipation, accompanied by some nerves as well. She paused at the edge of the door and took a deep breath before peering around the corner to see me. What she saw made her stomach feel like she'd been punched, and a grunt escaped her lips. Stopping dead in her tracks, she stared at the bolt still protruding from my head. Kate looked around anxiously for a nurse or doctor for a few moments before my nurse came with a few doctors from my surgery team.

"We're here to take him for surgery now," they let her know.

Breathing a deep sigh of relief, Kate bent to hold my hands and give me a kiss. "Good luck, honey," she said in parting, leaving for the night but planning to call when the surgery was over to hear the results.

Late that evening, she spoke to the nurse, who said, "Everything went well, and Kermit is responding to commands. We're going to give him some pain meds because his heart rate is a little high, but that's good because it means he should be out for the rest of the night, resting comfortably."

Why was the Twilight series such a thing in the United States? Why did I find *Sex God* such a compelling book? Why did Kate, Ali, Martha, and many others devote so much of their time, effort, and lives to thinking about me, praying for me, writing to me, coming to see me, and hanging out with me for hours on end?

I think it's because we're relational creatures made in the image of a relational God. This is part of what Jesus is getting at when He talks to the religious scholar in Luke 10 at the beginning of the chapter. When the man asked the Christ, "what do I need to do to get eternal life?" he was probably not asking about going to heaven. The lawyer was instead wondering what leads to a thriving and flourishing life here and now. In the Bible, eternal life is first and foremost a quality, not quantity, of life. It is life connected to the Divine here and now, in this moment. It's an existence full of joy, bliss, peace, grace, and love. Right here. Right now. Not one located in some far-off place or time, as we often imagine heaven to be, but heaven come to earth smack dab in the middle of all our mess, struggle, and pain.

What I'm getting at is tangible, loving relationships are the doorways to an amazing life. That's why we went gaga over the Twilight series. Who doesn't root for and rejoice over lovers coming together? And to make it vampire love, are you kidding me? Of course we divine image bearers would be thrilled by a passionate, romantic love that'll last forever. Relating this to the last chapter, and because I'm emphasizing the nowness of eternal life, I'll briefly pause to note I don't think heaven is now or later, but both now and *more* later.

An intimate, romantic relationship between two committed partners is, after all, perhaps the best human equivalent to the authenticity and vulnerability God desires with each of us and between us. This is why I think Rob Bell named his book *Sex God*. Sex is the most intimate of intimacies, wherein we most fully reveal ourselves to another, laying bare our entire being. Simultaneously, it's an act in which we most completely lose ourselves, as the borders and separation between lovers blurs and disappears. Sex, then, is both a full revealing of self and a complete losing of self. Whether or not we ever have sex, it symbolizes the level of 100 percent real connection we're made to enjoy with God, others, and ourselves, which means one could truthfully say we're meant to live sexy lives!

Deep, authentic, vulnerable love is the juice of life. When we share our lives with others, when we give our lives for others, when we care and are cared for, heaven comes to earth. Bliss fills our beings.

11

I Don't Know

> Just as you'll never understand the mystery of life forming in a pregnant woman, so you'll never understand the mystery at work in all that God does. (Ecclesiastes 11:5 The Message)

The older I get, the more I realize clichés and aphorisms speak truth. You know the old saying "Three steps forward, two steps back"? In many ways, that sums up my journey and sets the stage for this chapter.

Ali and Martha left on Sunday, leaving Kate largely alone again for a time. While en route to my room, Kate noticed that Donna was my nurse that day, which elicited a smile because Donna was exceptionally attentive to me. She would regularly stand and stare at me for long moments, but not in a creepy way. Instead, it was more of a fond, almost motherly regard, as if the power of her kind gaze itself could spur on my healing.

Upon seeing Kate, she gave a rundown on what I'd been up to and my current status. "Kermit's been a little slow moving and not very active, but he's been awake. He should be able to sit in the chair for a while, and we have physical therapy scheduled for today." With a hopeful expression on her face, Donna added, "It might not be too long before he is able to leave. Will you two come back and visit after he's better? We would really like that."

Kate nodded. "I bet we will, as soon as we have a chance, I'm guessing Lang will want to thank you all."

Dustin, from Bible study, came to visit that morning while I was sitting in the chair. Kate told him about Ali and Martha's visit and how much it'd meant to her to have them come from Tucson to see us and keep her and me company. She also gave a play-by-play of the most recent events in my stay in the ICU. At some point during their pleasant chat, Dustin handed Kate a card, after which they talked for a while longer. Eventually he rose, said he'd see us soon, gave her a hug, and left.

As Kate settled back into the chair, she opened the card. Gasping in shock, she found a timely and significant gift: five hundred dollars! She was jobless and taking care of me three states from her home, so this was like a gift from God to her. Eyes glistening, Kate discovered that Dustin and his wife, Hope, had felt a tug from the Creator, a feeling that they should do something to help Kate as she supported me. They determined to pray and listen to the Spirit separately and go from there. After being apart for a time to pray, they came back together and shared what the Divine had laid on their hearts. "I think God wants us to give Kate five hundred dollars," Dustin said with a degree of trepidation.

Mouth open in amazement at the power of God, Hope replied by saying she did too!

In Dustin's words, they felt God was using them "to give Kate a small breath of comfort." They understood the Source of Light and Love wanted them "to handle her smaller details so she could focus on helping and praying for me."

Kate sat in my room with the card in her hand for a long while. She was in awe of and praised God for the amazing love Dustin and Hope, as well as many others, had shown.

As the day wore on, I grew weaker and moved more slowly. As I tried to wave my arm toward Kate, it began shaking from exhaustion. Noticing I'd begun sweating while lying in bed in a room chilled to sixty-something degrees, Donna took my temperature: it read 101.5. For a regular healthy person, this would be troubling but not concerning. Given my severely weakened condition, it was both, and it carried with it an important question: Was this just from a minor illness, or was it something more major?

That evening, Misha was my nurse. She'd been my nurse the first night I was in the hospital. After being in my room a few times and looking me over, she told Kate, "I think Kermit is getting a lung infection." She went on to note I was feverish and had a bad smell coming from my breathing tube, as if something was rancid.

The next morning, I lay asleep with my back propped up in bed, but my head was slumped to the slide. Anxious to determine whether the day was going to be good or bad, Kate began softly prodding me with her hands. Fortunately for my fiancée, I generally wake up in a good mood, without the grumpiness that she and many others usually experience. I looked into her eyes as if to say, "Okay, I'm up, dear. What would you like?"

"Can you see me?" she queried.

I gave her thumbs-up.

Kate followed that with, "Are you feeling okay?"

I turned my hand on its side and waved it back and forth. "Kind of."

"Look, Lang, I'm wearing your Seahawks sweatshirt." She pointed to her clothes.

I slowly reached my hand out to her in appreciation.

"It's Sunday, football day. Are you going to watch football with me today?"

I nodded. Then a moment later, I fell asleep.

I slept most of the day but woke up for short periods of time fairly often. However, during these moments of "consciousness," I was back to having the blank expression in my eyes from the Thanksgiving setback, when there was too much brain fluid in my head. What was more, I barely moved around, and when I did, it was slowly. Testing the waters, during one of my waking moments, Kate said, "Give me a thumbs-up if you remember who I am, Lang."

Gazing dully in the distance, I did nothing.

Concerned, Kate passed what she'd observed on to the hospital staff. "I've noticed that since the shunt surgery, Lang has seemed to regress again. He's not scooting around the bed. He hasn't smiled. He barely moves. I'm worried about him."

My high temperature from the previous day made the workers worried I might have an infection, so they measured my white blood cell count. Typically, when someone has an infection, he produces extra white blood cells, so the count becomes elevated. The test came back indicating I was in the normal range, so it appeared I didn't have an infection.

This didn't alleviate Kate's anxiety. At her wits' end after my rollercoaster ride of ups and downs, she went to a doctor looking for some answers. After spotting one involved with my recovery and familiar with my case, Kate set in with a stream of question.

"What's going on with Lang? When are we going to know what's wrong? Why does he keep having all these ups and downs? Is he going to recover and be like he was before? Why is he sometimes his old self, and sometimes he seems gone?"

With sympathetic eyes and a friendly smile, the doctor replied with wise words that I think apply not just to medicine but to much of life. "If we knew everything, they would call it perfect medicine. There is a reason they call it practicing medicine."

Although this made logical sense to Kate's mind, it didn't land in her heart. Perhaps rationality is not the language of our souls, unable to calm a troubled heart like a hug does. Heavy with fears and questions, Kate sat by my bed and poured her heart out to God and me by praying, journaling, and speaking the following lament.

"I really miss you. Won't you please come back to me? I would love to see you scooting around to get comfy, throwing your legs off the bed, or trying to sit up. Since the surgery on Friday, you haven't done that ... Please, God, just show me a sign that Lang is going to be okay."

When Dr. O checked in on us that evening, I woke up and intently listened to his conversation with Kate. "Do you want me to explain what we're talking about?" Kate asked me.

Falling Into Love

I gave her thumbs-up. "You're going to get transferred from the ICU to a rehab hospital soon. Today is Sunday, and depending on how well you do, we could leave as soon as Tuesday. It looks like we're almost certainly going to Palo Alto, California."

While she talked, I moved around, putting my arms behind my head and then on my chest. Then I reached for her. I scooted around on the bed a bit, moving my legs to reposition myself in a more comfortable manner. I was more active than I'd been since the surgery, and I was moving at a more normal speed. As Kate looked me over, she noted that my right eye still wasn't opening; it hadn't since the accident. First it had been swollen shut, but even after it, healed it hadn't opened at all.

All my resting on Sunday seemed to pay dividends Monday. I had enough energy to finish multiple sessions of PT, repeatedly lifting my arms and legs to regain strength and range of motion. After nearly a month of being largely bedridden and sometimes fighting for my life, my condition was such that a "good" day of exhausting PT for me was a few repetitions of morning stretches for regular folks.

In between sessions, I was alert and interested enough to ask Kate to talk to me and remind me what was going on. She went over the events of the accident to refresh my memory as to what happened and why I was in the hospital. After bringing me up to date, she concluded with, "Dr. O is going to put your feeding tube in tonight. Then tomorrow you'll rest, and we should be going to Palo Alto for rehab on Wednesday December 10."

When Kate was around and I wasn't doing PT or getting caught up on things by her, she frequently read to me. That day, she began on *Jesus Wants to Save the Christians*, a book about the exodus story from the time of Moses and how Jesus was the ultimate fulfillment of not only Israel's exodus from slavery and oppression but also all exoduses from the powers that trick us, bind us, or enslave us to their causes to this day. I stared at Kate and kept crossing and uncrossing my legs while she read.

As often happened, when the nurses passed by the room, they would stop and gaze in at us for a while. In the midst of her reading, Kate looked up to see four nurses standing outside the room, smiling, and looking in at us.

Grinning at what had been a day of steps in the right direction, Kate left for dinner with the understanding I'd have surgery in the evening. Later that night, Dr. O put my feeding tube in via a simple surgical procedure, and Kate took her first night off from the hospital since we'd arrived.

Tuesday witnessed further progress forward. The doctors removed the splints from both of my wrists. I still had my jaw wired shut and a neck brace, but the jaw was scheduled for freedom in a couple days. The neck would stay confined for about three weeks so it could finish healing. As exciting as these positive steps were, the most encouraging part of the day was when I walked, with help, for the first time in a long while. Weakened and in poor shape, I managed only a few steps and couldn't stand fully erect. Instead of a regular, healthy person's stroll, think more in terms of the feeble, slouched-over shuffle of the walking dead (i.e., a zombie) supported by people on either side. Still, it was quite encouraging to everyone.

The final details of my transfer seemed to be falling into place. I would take a fifteen-thousand-dollar airborne ambulance, or Air Evac, to Palo Alto on Friday, December 12, my birthday. I could have left earlier, but Dr. O felt it best to be cautious, and he had some concerns. "Kate, I'm worried about Lang's lungs. It looks like he may be getting pneumonia. We'll do some more tests to find out. I don't want him transferred before he's ready because then there's the possibility he'll take a few major steps back. He should be able to leave on Friday, but he still has a fever, and that needs to be gone for twenty-four hours before he can depart. The VA hospital in Palo Alto requires he be under 100.3 for a day before he transfers."

On Wednesday morning, my jaw wires were finally removed, and better still, I was fever free. However, the doctors noticed my left pupil was extremely large, so they called in Dr. O for his opinion.

He examined me for a minute, not liking that I'd began a shaking fit again. He quickly determined another CAT scan was in order, along with a sedative for the tremors. The results of the scan indicated a change in the fluid in my brain, but the doctors were unsure of the cause. Thus, Dr. Smith, the neurosurgeon, was paged to review the CAT scan. "It looks fine," he said after examination. "But we should have neurology look it over to be sure. Also, Lang's shaking makes me want another EEG to be sure he's not having the kind of seizures that would concern us."

As the sun began descending on Las Vegas, Kate found out the EEG indicated I was fine—no seizures of the troubling variety. Soon after this, Pastor Doug came by. As I noticed him walk through my door, excitement erupted on my face. I immediately, like a slow-moving and uncoordinated zombie would, sat up, and extended my hand for a shake. I paid close attention and watched him throughout his entire stay, as if some part of me knew there was a mysterious sacredness in the air.

"I prayed for Lang on the way in," Pastor Doug told Kate, "and God told me to read him this scripture, Psalm 37. 'Delight yourself in the LORD; And He will give you the desires of your heart.... When he falls, he will not be hurled headlong, because the LORD is the One who holds his hand. I have been young and now I am old, yet I have not seen the righteous forsaken ... But the salvation of the righteous is from the LORD; He is their strength in time of trouble. The LORD helps them and delivers them; He delivers them from the wicked and saves them, because they take refuge in Him.'"

Speaking of being delivered from the wicked, one of the odder and grosser ailments that afflicted me as a result of the accident revealed itself after my jaw wires were taken out; I'd caught thrush. Thrush is a yeast infection in the mouth or throat. It causes white spots to appear. Kate said that it got so bad that it looked like a forest had grown in my mouth.

That night Matt, a best friend, arrived from Tucson. We'd met about seven years before in Tucson, connecting with each other through a church because we were both interested in being in a small group. I'd moved across town in Tucson in the autumn of 2001 and began looking for a church. After trying a few, I found Casas and went for their young adult focused gathering. Matt, bald with a goatee, was onstage leading worship. As he played guitar, sang, and danced, his passion spilled out into the crowd, lifting us all into more intimate celebration of God. To make a long story short, I love music, and Matt's heart-felt worship was the primary reason I decided to regularly attend Casas. It wasn't long before I inquired about joining a small group, got linked up with Matt, and became fast friends with him.

He worked in IT and enjoyed most things computer related; our shared love of technology and computer games was one of our bonding points. At the time of his visit, his company was closing down in the very near future, meaning he was looking for a job. Yet in the midst of that major time of transition, he still made a trip up to see me in the hospital for a few days.

On Thursday morning, Matt walked in for a visit to see me sitting in the chair, where I stayed for three and a half hours! As odd as it may sound, this was a big deal and the equivalent of intense exercise for me. Pretty crazy, don't you think?

With my buddy visiting, time to spare, and finally being free of my jaw wires, I tried to talk but couldn't generate the volume to get out comprehensible words. My full-volume speech was as intelligible and loud as a bee buzzing. So like before, Kate had me write things out by hand.

"I need water," was what I scrawled first. My fiancée quickly poured me a cup. I followed it up with, "Stretch my head, please."

"I'm sure your neck is really stiff, my dear," Kate soothed. "You have a neck brace on, so I can't reach it. It'll come off in a few weeks."

While I sat with Matt and Kate talking to me, various doctors and nurses made sure to stop by, knowing I was scheduled to leave the next day. "Goodbye, Kermit. Please come visit after you're recovered. We'd love to see you."

After my long stint in the chair, I was worn out and went to sleep. Kate and Matt sat nearby and got to know each other better. Matt shared some, but Kate shared a lot, both painting a good sketch of her overall life story and focusing mainly on our time together. For instance, she told him the tale of our magical night at the Bellagio in Las Vegas.

In the quiet moments, Matt sat by my side with his hand on my knee or hand. At times he was silent, and sometimes he softly hummed (quite possibly Dave Matthews Band songs because they are his favorite band too, and we'd gone to several of their concerts together). His heart ached because of my broken state. Although I was getting better, I looked like a mess. I was rail thin, my hair looked like a zombie mad scientist (my head was shaved on the top and normal length on the sides and back), I wore a neck brace, I bore scars from surgeries in multiple places (including a long, prominent one stretching from the top of my forehead to the back of my skull), and my muscles had virtually withered away. Matt sat, happy to be with me and glad to get to know Kate, yet he had a deep sadness in his eyes.

Later in the day came bad news. One of the staff members delivered it to Kate. "I'm sorry, but Kermit isn't going to be able to leave tomorrow. His temperature has gone back above the threshold. We're not sure what's wrong, so we're going to have an infectious disease specialist come check him."

On my thirty-fourth birthday, December 12, I greeted Matt and Kate with a temperature of 102.9. Jerri Ann, my nurse, gave me some Tylenol for the fever, which got my temperature down to 101.5. However, it soon climbed all the way to 103. Because she couldn't give me more Tylenol, my nurse then decided to put two ice bags under my armpits. This did stop my temperature from climbing, but it didn't have the desired result of cooling me off.

Matt came up with a creative way to solve my temperature problem. "I should just blow some cool air up Lang's skirt to make his temperature go down!" Leave it to Matt to bring some humor to a frustrating situation by jesting about the semiexposed state my hospital gown left me in.

Jerri Ann was talking to Kate and Matt about my fever and other issues when she let slip the phrase "Pooping in high cotton."

My friend and fiancée burst into laughter. "I don't know what that means, but it's funny," Kate concluded.

By way of explanation, Jerri Ann offered, "Hey, I'm from Texas."

Concerned by my rising temperature, the doctors ordered a chest X-ray. This led to their discovery of my fever's cause, a lot of fluid around my right lung. My birthday present from the hospital was a chest tube to drain the buildup. That day alone, it sucked out 600 cc, or 0.63 quarts, of liquid—the equivalent of a glass of water. The effects were pretty immediate: my temperature temporarily fell to 101. To ease my pain, the doctor gave me a sizeable dose of morphine, sending me into a peaceful slumber for the rest of the day beginning around 5:00 p.m.

That evening, Dr. O gave Kate and Matt a rundown of the latest events and their effects. "I don't think an infection caused the fluid in the lungs. Kermit probably had a tear in his right lung that couldn't be detected, and it slowly leaked, filling up his right lung with fluid. The fluid we drained from his lung had blood in it, which indicates it's from trauma. We'll be able to take the tube out when it drains less than 100 cc in a twenty-four-hour period. With a chest tube now, he can't be transported by air for two weeks after it's removed. I'm guessing we'll be able to take the tube out in three to four days, so we'll probably just transport him on the ground via ambulance."

To celebrate my birthday, Kate brought the hospital staff treats, mouthwatering cupcakes from The Cupcakery, which, she later told me, were "sinfully delicious." These tasty, large treats come in a variety of flavors, such as red velvet with cream cheese frosting, chocolate peanut butter cup, and maple syrup cake with pecans topped with pecan cream cheese frosting. Needless to say, the cupcakes were a huge hit with the caregivers.

My temperature had gone down from the high of 103, but it continued to hover in the 101–102 range. I spent a lot of the day sleeping, and while I was awake, Kate and Matt chatted me up. "Hey, Lang, I have to go back home to Ali and the kids on Sunday," Matt said.

Realizing I had no time to waste, I pantomimed with my hands like I was writing with a pen, so Kate gave me a pen and paper. "What are the plans for the weekend?" I asked. While lying in bed with a fever, I was concerned with not only what my future in the hospital was but how Matt, Kate, and I would find entertainment.

Laughing at my perpetual planning nature, Kate replied, "The plan is to wait—wait for your fever to go down, wait for you to be stable enough to transfer, wait for the doctors to figure out why you have the reoccurring fever. Wait, that's the plan. Wait." Smiling, she added, "I think *wait* is a new four-letter word to me. What would you like to do while we wait?"

Kate rattled off a few options for us. I gave double thumbs-up to watching a movie on the laptop, listening to my audiobooks, and bringing in some music.

"Peggy," Kate said to my nurse, "can I ask you a favor?"

"Sure," Peggy answered.

"Lang is looking like a mad scientist with his head shaved on the top, combined with poofy and curly hair on the sides. Can you shave it to be even?"

Peggy gladly set about making me a little less freakish looking, quickly shaving all my hair the same short length. Satisfied with my new look, Kate told me I looked "handsome."

Just because I looked a bit better didn't mean I felt better, though. I continued to emphasize to Kate how much my neck brace bothered me. I even tried to take it off.

"No, Lang," Kate insisted.

After waving for a pen and paper, I scrawled, "Kate, defend me!" indicating I felt that if she really had my best interest in mind, she'd let me take off the brace.

She repeated that she couldn't let me do that. Frustrated, I shook my head angrily, scowled, and pointed at first Kate and then the door.

"You want me to leave?" my fiancée wondered.

I nodded my head. However, mere minutes later, I reached for her hand, pulled it to my lips, and began gently kissing her fingers. With the brain injury, I was, and would continue to be, prone to fits of emotion. Fortunately, though, at the center of my community and the core of my being were, and are, Christ and love, which meant I always had a stable home to return to.

A few days later, we'd reached mid-December, the fifteenth, and I was still in the ICU. At various points earlier in my stay, I could have left if decisions had been timelier or slightly different. If the air force hadn't taken so long determining where I'd go for inpatient rehab, or if Dr. O had been less cautious, I'd have been long gone from the Vegas ICU. Fortunately, and quite possibly because of the prayers of Kate, Matt, and hundreds of others, that was not the case. This meant I was in the capable hands of Dr. O and his crew while I battled the fever, stemming from what they were now becoming convinced was an infection.

The heart and lung specialist came in and examined my lung just before dinnertime. "We're going to put a second tube in," he explained to Kate. "The first chest tube isn't reaching all the fluid. We'll put the second one in from a different angle. The situation might call for surgery, but hopefully this next tube will prevent that."

In went the second tube into my right lung, and out came a brownish black liquid that filled the room with a puke smell. There was now no doubt my lung was infected. They took a sample of the infected fluid to test so they could identify the infection and give me an antibiotic specifically tailored to fight it. A chest X-ray taken after the tube insertion showed a clear improvement, but surgery was still a possibility.

Around 7:30 p.m., during nonvisiting hours and while Kate was gone for dinner, my temperature spiked. When she got back to the hospital, it had barely gone down ... to a still shocking just below 105. Fearful and on the verge of a tearful breakdown, Kate sent a text to all her friends and family asking for quick prayer. After three hours of Tylenol, ice packs, cold compresses, and prayer, my heat had dropped to a still worrisome but not so scary 103 degrees.

Upon leaving the hospital that evening, Kate checked her phone. Pastor Doug had heard Kate's plea for prayers and sent her a quote from Matthew 7:7 to lift her spirits. "Ask and it will be given to you; seek and you will find; knock and the door will be opened for you" (New International Version).

When Kate entered my room the next morning, she found me sitting in my chair.

"Good morning," I greeted her cheerfully. Neal, the speech therapist, had given me a valve for my trach, which allowed me to talk again. What was more, as the sun was rising that morning, my fever had fallen to 101 degrees.

Neal had talked to me for a while before Kate arrived, so he gave her the scoop on my current state of mind. "Kermit seems good but a little loopy," he said with a smile. "It could be the fever or all the drugs, but it's common for head injuries." With a slight chuckle and an "all is well" tone, Neal continued the tale. "He thinks it's 1998. All head patients lose years in increments of ten, but he'll get them back. It was funny; he said your name was Miranda. When the nurse asked him if it was actually Kate, he said that was your nickname. He added that you lived in Canada, and he lived in Tucson."

Eager to please, I provided Kate with some more humor as I played with a wet washcloth. I put it in my mouth, sucked on it, and then rubbed it all over my face. Then I placed it on my forehead and leaned back, content. I repeated this process with different variations numerous times while Kate sat in her chair, chortling quietly.

On December 17, it snowed in Las Vegas a lot, at least for the area. Not only did it snow in the desert, a quite unusual occurrence, but it snowed enough to close the airport. I take it as a sign that it was a weird year: a guy slipped, slid, and fell off a cliff in a totally inexplicable event. It snowed where it almost never snows. The Seattle SuperSonics moved to Oklahoma City and became the Thunder. Life is sometimes strange. Fortunately, the airport didn't close until after Kate picked up Leif and Tarrah, her sister, a tall woman who looks like Kate, brown haired with great dimples and a brilliant smile.

After picking up her family from the airport, Kate brought them by the hospital for about an hour. I grinned and squeezed Leif's hand when he came in. The doctor met with Kate and said, "The most recent CAT scan of his chest was really good. It showed substantial improvement; there's only a small pocket of fluid left."

Once again, I was on the upswing, but why? Why did I keep getting better only to then take steps back, leaving those near and dear to me on pins and needles as to what would become or remain of Lang when all was said and done? Why did I survive this severe trauma when many other people die from less dire injuries? Why did Dustin and Hope feel moved to give money to Kate, and why had Pastor Doug heard a nudge to share Psalm 37? Why did I, a risk-averse guy, fall off a cliff during a family friendly hike in the first place?

I have thoughts and beliefs on all these topics. I have ideas that make sense and meaning of life and ultimate reality. As you've likely noticed, throughout this book, I've been sharing many of my views on such matters. The truth is although I believe love is what saved and healed me, our Creator endlessly seeks to embrace everyone, and that God spoke to and through Dustin, Hope, and Pastor Doug. The truth is I don't know what's behind the curtain, so to speak.

I emphasize my not knowing and find it to be a helpful stance for a few reasons. It helps me engage the great mysteries of life from a humble place of awe and wonder. After all, how can a mere human claim to fully grasp subjects like God, infinity, trauma and tragedy, death, the universe, love, or beauty? I don't think these are categories we can definitively or completely know or get, so much as they are infinitely knowable.

Falling Into Love

Simply consider the Divine for a second. How could we possibly either prove or disprove God? Our Creator isn't an object we can study and be certain of. Instead, the Trinity is a subject we experience and relate to. Philosophers say God isn't so much a being but is instead the ground of Being itself. All I'm saying is I have experiences of light, love, and beauty I believe are Divine encounters ... yet I could be wrong.

Additionally, I find this stance leads to a more authentic expression of faith. Despite what I learned for much of my life, as I understand it now, faith is not an intellectual belief. It's not affirming certain doctrines in my head. It's not being intellectually certain there is a God, we'll continue on after we die, or the overall arch of the universe is bending toward goodness. Instead, faith is *trusting* in Truths we aren't certain of. It's living into realities we can't prove.

Finally, the less I claim to be certain of, the more space I leave and create for others to have their own unique, beautiful, and diverse understanding of life, the universe, and everything. When I live with less certainty and smaller amounts of intellectual clinging, my heart becomes simultaneously more spacious and full of love. What's more, it opens the door for me and friends, family, acquaintances, and strangers to learn and grow from each other.

As a side note, not knowing is a very restful place. The less I claim to know, the less I have to defend, posture, or argue. It leaves more room for peace, joy, and connection.

Let me also mention that I write this as much for myself as I do for you. It's quite easy for me to default to a stance of certainty and superiority. Truly, the less we know, the more we live and love ... and even though I've tasted the fruits of this, I'm still working at living it!

12

A Christmas to Remember

Kind words heal and help; cutting words wound and maim. (Proverbs 15:4 The Message)

On December 19, I got to eat again after I passed my swallow evaluation with the speech therapist—a test to make sure I could swallow food without choking. I slowly lifted graham crackers to my mouth, washing them down with lemon water. Then I was given chocolate pudding. I took a bite and sat there with a blissful expression on my face.

"Why aren't you swallowing the pudding, Lang?" Kate wondered.

"Because it tastes so good." After thoroughly enjoying the pleasure of being able to actually eat, I asked Kate, "Where is Lara?"

"She's with Amy," Kate answered.

"Are you sure?" I pressed for no discernable reason other than the weird behaviors associated with my traumatic brain injury.

Smiling, Kate said, "Yes, I talked to her a couple of days ago."

Remembering my memory issues, my speech therapist asked me, "Do you know who that is?" pointing toward Kate.

With no hesitation, I gave my response. "My beautiful, future bride."

Beaming with pleasure, Kate told me, "Now that you can eat, I can get you some food. What would you like me to bring you?"

Immediately my mind went to Red Robin and one of my favorite foods in the world. "Onion rings!" There are few things I enjoy eating more.

The next day, I was not so energetic. Kate asked me if I wanted to go for a walk.

"No, I'm tired."

"You sure you don't want to go for a walk?" she persisted.

"No, I'll do it later," I replied with a louder voice.

With pauses, this exchange continued for a few minutes. Each time, I raised my volume a little more. However, given my weakened condition and raw voice, I wasn't exactly scary or intimidating; Kate actually found it cute. Knowing she wasn't going to convince me to go for a walk by being straightforward, Kate hit upon a more subtle method. "Lang, did you know that Christmas is only five days away? What do you want for Christmas?"

Grinning and gazing into her eyes, I paused before simply saying, "You."

"Do you want to know what I want for Christmas, Lang?"

"Yes," I nodded.

"What I want is for the two of us to take a walk down the hallway by ourselves on Christmas Day. You only have five days to practice this task, so you should get to it."

Sighing, I caved in. "Okay, let's take a walk."

It took Kate and three nurses to help support me and take care of all the tubes, wires, and machines hooked to me. After what seemed like hours to me, we'd made it only a few steps outside my room before I showed considerable signs of fatigue. Along with my entourage of helpers and scads of medical devices, I made the ponderous turn to head back to my cozy confines.

As we settled back into my room, Kate looked at my exhausted form sink into bed and raised her eyebrow. "How was the walk?"

"It sucked."

Laughing and holding her stomach, Kate said, "I can see how it would suck. I appreciate you doing it for me, though."

"You're welcome," I grumbled in her direction.

"Lang, I'm so proud of you. You're getting healthier, and I think you're much closer to transferring. Walking every day is going to

Falling Into Love

help with that. You still have a low-grade fever, the fluid in your lung, and arm tremors, but you've come so far. I'm sure you'll overcome the remaining obstacles."

That night, Kevin, a best friend, and his fiancée, Sarah, came from Tucson to relieve Tarrah at Kate's side. Kevin, a pastor at the time, and I had met through a young men's group at church when I lived in Tucson. One of our favorite pastimes was to watch college basketball, particularly when the University of Arizona (Kevin's team) played Washington State University or the University of Washington (my teams). We shared an overwhelming passion to follow Jesus, and we helped encourage each other to new levels in this pursuit.

Sarah is the light of Kevin's life and one of the cutest women I've ever met, graced with dazzling dimples and an inner brightness that shines through. She is blunt and straightforward in the kindest of ways, meaning what you see is what you get. Not only do I admire and appreciate her authenticity, but to top it off, she loves wine, a passion I share with her.

Sunday, Kate and Kevin walked a little down the hall with me. That afternoon, she went back to Julie's house to spend mother-son time with Leif for the rest of the day, as well as all the next. With Kevin and Sarah in town to watch over me and keep me company, Kate took a well-deserved daylong break from my bedside for the first time in a month and a half. That evening, Kevin and Sarah got me to walk a second time for the day, farther down the hall then I'd been before.

The next day, while Kate enjoyed a well-deserved day off, I set a personal record and walked all the way down the hall (a good seventy-five feet) and back. I got an encouraging fist bump from Kevin for my achievement. Even better, my fever was gone, at least by ICU standards. I was right around 101, so I still needed to reach 100.3 to be "fever free" according to Palo Alto. I also needed to have my chest tubes removed before I could switch hospitals.

Compared to everything I'd been through, the smallness of these last steps I had to take had us in a festive mood when Christmas rolled around. My mom, Kathy, and stepdad, Rick, came to Vegas on Christmas Eve, so until Kevin and Sarah left on the twenty-fifth, I had quite a crowd to visit with: Kate, my mom, Rick, Kevin, and Sarah. (Leif flew back on the twenty-third to spend Christmas with his dad).

"Merry Christmas," everyone said to me the morning of the twenty-fifth as they walked into my room. It was decked out with red, green, Santa Claus, and as much Christmas stuff as Kevin, Sarah, and Kate could get into my space without interfering with the machines and people keeping me healthy.

Unable to contain herself, Kate took my hand and asked, "Lang, do you remember what my Christmas wish was?"

"Yes ... walk," I said to my devoted fiancée.

"Are you ready to give me my Christmas wish now?" she asked as she squealed with joy and grinned liked she'd won the lottery.

"Yes," I smiled in her direction.

Kate and Kevin helped me get slowly out of bed, clad in my hospital gown. I stood a bit shakily, with Kate on my right and Kevin on my left. After taking a deep breath, I said I was ready to make a holiday wish come true.

Hand in hand with Kate, with her other arm under my shoulder and Kevin's arm around my waist, we proceeded from the room. With calves so skinny an adult could wrap a hand around one, I slowly but determinedly placed one foot in front of the other. All the while, I leaned on my companions for much-needed support. *Shuffle, shuffle* went my feet as we proceeded down the hall. Partway through, we paused for pictures to record this joyful moment.

After a couple breaks for me to rest, we made it halfway down the hall. Upon turning around, we proceeded back to my room, and all the while Kate kept squeezing my hand, smiling, and telling me how appreciative she was of her Christmas present.

That wasn't the only present I had for my fiancée that day, thanks to the loving support of my family. After Kevin and Sarah left to celebrate the day with their family, Kate stepped out of the room for a few moments. When she returned, I sat in my bed holding a card toward her. While Kate looked at me with confusion, Rick said, "It's a card for you from Lang, Kate."

A shiver of joy ran down Kate's spine as she giggled with glee. I had signed the card, "Love, Lang," myself. What was more, inside was a picture of Kate's Christmas present from me: a karaoke machine. Before the accident, I had told Leia that I'd seen a karaoke machine at Costco I was thinking of getting Kate for Christmas. She loved karaoke, dancing around, making hand motions, singing, and so on. Basically, Kate loved the performance, fun, and crazy part of karaoke. She repeatedly said she couldn't sing, but she didn't care. Remembering our conversation, Leia decided it'd be cool to have the family get the karaoke machine for Kate from me.

She wrapped her arms around me and held me tight. "I love you. Thank you, thank you, thank you," she said blissfully.

My family, friends, and Kate had one more reason to be thankful on Christmas: my temperature stayed below 100.3 the entire day. Their holiday cheer grew even brighter based on the very real prospect that I'd soon be leaving the ICU to begin preparing and rehabilitating for a new chapter in life.

The good news continued, and life became a bit more normal for me the next day, when the staff took off my neck brace. Stretching my head from side to side, I sighed in contentment. After a while, my people did voice some signs of concern because my head leaned some to the right when I sat or stood, but the nurses said that was normal and would get worked out as I strengthened my neck. It was almost like I was a baby learning to support his head with my own strength.

Although I was eating some regular food (only things soft and easy to chew), the vast majority of my sustenance still needed to come through my feeding tube. That said, to gradually prepare me for eating more regular food as part of meals, the dietician changed my feeding tube regime. He switched me from a slow, continuous supply of food to larger amounts every few hours. The goal was to begin getting my stomach used to eating on a regular schedule again.

I didn't react very well to this change. As Kate, my mom, and Rick were sitting in the room, my stomach heaved. I fought to close my mouth, but a stream of partially digested food erupted from my lips in projectile fashion, spewing across the room. Rick quickly grabbed my mom's arm and hurried her from the room to short-circuit any sympathetic reaction. Kate, meanwhile, sat in relief because I had just barely missed her.

Although my fever was gone and my lungs were mostly clear, I was still not ready to leave. "We think there is a clot in his lung. It's preventing the fluid from completely draining. We're going to insert medicine into his lung to attempt to break up the clot and get the rest of his fluid to drain. We'll take a CAT scan tonight to get a better idea of how much more fluid is left and make a determination as to whether we'll need to perform surgery," one of the doctors told my people.

The CAT scan revealed good progress in my right lung. Unfortunately, it also revealed there wasn't just one cot—there were several to break up. Still, the fluid was noticeably diminished from the last viewing. The only real bad news was the doctors were still unsure whether they'd need to conduct surgery to fully heal my lung.

Saturday, December 27, was my forty-seventh day in the ICU. By that point, as much as the staff truly wanted me to be able to leave, they'd grown so attached to me that they knew parting would be both joyful and sorrowful. Along those lines, one of the nurses shared the following with Kate.

"I just want you to know that without you even knowing, you have impacted my life in a large way. During your time of suffering and struggle, your big heart aided me through a hard time in my life. Your words of encouragement and courage in the face of adversary have inspired me to be strong and persevere through my own dark night. I thank you more than you will ever know."

On a more lighthearted but no less grateful note, another nurse excitedly told my family, "We think that Kermit might break the record for longest stay in the ICU. The longest one we've found is fifty-four days." They began rooting for me to set a new mark.

I was strong enough to go on short walks twice a day, so the staff took the opportunity to weigh me. I checked in at six feet tall and 124 pounds. There was not much to me aside from skin and bones.

With that in mind, Kate took it as her mission to put some meat back on my body. She found the key: chocolate peanut butter ice cream from Coldstone. As she fed me the milkshake version of this deliciousness, my eyes widened in pleasure, and my one-track mind could do nothing but focus on the yummy goodness entering my mouth.

As odd as it may sound, at that point I had some problems swallowing food. I couldn't move the muscles to effectively swallow it because I had forgotten how. This problem continued for several weeks, but there was no issue with the milkshake—I slurped it down in a hurry. Grinning with a pleasure that only chocolate and peanut butter combined can give (peanut butter cups are my favorite candy), I shot Kate a thumbs-up.

"As long as you keep up the good work in eating, Lang, I'll bring you a milkshake every day," Kate promised.

As I made my way down the hall that day, my mom strolled behind me. I had on my hospital gown and scrubs-style trousers. As my legs shuffled back and forth, they jarred my pants loose, which slipped, slid, and fell down to the floor, leaving my bum exposed. My mom, gazing my direction as we moved, desperately tried to avert her eyes, but she was not in time. She'd been mooned by her son!

Feeling better and better, the second time I went for a walk on Saturday, I shambled my feet down the hall as quickly as possible. "He made it down the seventy-five-foot hall in sixty seconds," Rick reported. Add that to having no tremors or fever that day, and it seemed we were on the last legs of our stay in the ICU.

The only problem remaining was the clots in my right lung,

which were preventing the fluid from being fully drained. After analyzing the situation, on Monday (day forty-nine in the hospital), the staff called in a cardio doctor. He used a CAT scan to guide in a smaller tube, behind the clot that had resisted all efforts to break it up. If this didn't work, they were fairly certain they'd need a surgery to finish the job, which they wanted to avoid if possible.

"I'm confident this new tube will resolve the issue," the cardio doctor told my people.

Afterward, I went for a walk with Kate, my mom, and Rick, as had become my daily routine. Each time I grew more confident, raised my feet higher off the ground, shuffled less, stood more upright, and needed less support from my escorts. I got to the end of the hall, and then I kept going. I walked all the way to the hospital's door and went outside! For the first time in forty-nine days, I took a breath of fresh, crisp, nonhospital air. I breathed in and out, stuck my thumbs up in celebration, looked around for a couple of seconds, and shivered.

Kate stood by my side, marveling at the healing power of love. Specifically, the others-oriented, life-giving, caring, encouraging, and transformative divine love of God and people working together in blessed community. She audibly thanked God for saving my life and bringing so many incredible people into our lives. Looking my way, she paused and, with a tear, added how much she admired my strength.

Although it was a truly magical moment, I was still not well enough to enjoy very much enchantment. Thus, after a brief pause to take in everything, I turned to go back inside. In my defense, on top of my still poor health, it barely broke fifty degrees in Las Vegas that day, and I was clad only in a gown.

Like eating, another odd after effect of my accident on things we take for granted was my inability to talk. The doctors had done all the things required for me to speak, and I had previously talked at various points in the ICU. However, by December 30, when I tried to speak, nothing would come out. The speech therapist came by to try to get me to talk and judge my verbal comprehension by asking questions. "He understands what I say," she explained to Kate. "He just can't get the words out." She talked about how my brain needed to build new connections for speaking, adding she was "hopeful Kermit will make a full recovery."

She concluded by explaining to Kate and my mom how they could help my brain remap itself. "Sing him songs that he would know." My mom and Kate began performing tunes they were positive I'd recognize, things like "Ba Ba Black Sheep," "ABCs," "Happy Birthday," and "Jesus Loves Me." I applaud the ladies for playing it safe, but couldn't they have chosen some cool adult songs, like tunes from Dave Matthews Band or U2?

On my stroll that evening, I set another milestone. For the first time, I walked most of the long white hall on my own! Aside from a bit of assistance from the nurses and Kate here and there, I relied only on a walker and my strength to make the trek. Since I was still hooked up to multiple machines, though, the nurses guided them along in my wake, it was like a macabre wedding procession.

I make that observation because the first day of the next year, January 1, 2009, was supposed to be an amazing day that changed Kate and my lives forever. It was our planned wedding day. As she sat beside me that afternoon, in a voice flavored with reflectiveness, gratitude, sadness, heartache, and joy, my fiancée softly said, "Today is our wedding day. Thirty minutes from now, I would be walking down the aisle, and we would be saying, 'I do.' Thirty minutes from now, I would be Mrs. Lang Charters. I refuse to be sad today, but disappointment keeps creeping in."

As Kate sat in my room trying not to think about what we had planned to be doing, the sounds of the hospital washed over her. The beeps and squeaks of the various machines connected to me. The low talking of nurses and doctors filtered down the hall. Then a long, piercing howl of pain echoed through the halls, eventually tapering out, but only to be intermittently repeated for some time. The lady she heard expressed an agony that Kate realized could have been hers if my accident had turned out differently: the death of her husband. "Thank you, God, for saving Lang," Kate prayed through wet eyes.

After I'd had three tubes for a few days, the doctors ordered another CAT scan to determine how well the fluid was draining. On day fifty-three of my time in the ICU, most of it was gone, and the doctors were so pleased with this progress that they removed two of my chest tubes. One clot remained stubborn, blocking the drainage of the last bit of fluid, so they pumped some liquid onto the clot to dissolve it.

I continued trying to talk, with little to show for it. "How do you feel with two of your tubes out, dear?" Kate asked.

My jaw worked up and down, but all that came out was a faint, indistinguishable whisper. My lips formed the words correctly, but unfortunately Kate didn't know how to read lips.

The nurses brought in some food for me, but it seems I'd recently decided I didn't really want to eat. Trying to break me out of this funk and put some weight on me, Kate helped me put some pudding in my mouth. I swallowed a little at first. Then I sat there with my food in my mouth. Apparently, I had decided that I was done eating midbite and that, in my brain-injury-induced, sometimes childlike state, the best way to get rid of the remaining food was to spit it at Kate. Thus ended all efforts to try to get me to eat that day.

Occasionally, when I attempted to talk, a word, phrase, or sentence would escape my lips in a normal voice. "I'm in pain," I told Tim, my nurse, on Saturday morning. Perhaps my vocal cords decided to cooperate only when it was really important.

That was my fifty-fourth day in the ICU, which the staff initially thought would tie the record for longest stay. However, we found out a lady who had been in a plane crash and had been burned severely, had actually stayed considerably longer. Still, reaching second place for longest stay in the ICU was a testament to how many issues the doctors, nurses, and other staff had to overcome to get me well.

As I got a chest X-ray to determine the effectiveness of the remaining tube that day, Kate waited anxiously for the results. Dr. O walked in with a smile on his face. "Kate, Lang's lung looks healthy. The fluid is drained. We will remove the last tube tomorrow. We'll monitor him for a few days, and as long as nothing goes wrong, you'll then be on your way to Palo Alto."

On day fifty-five in the ICU, not only did I get my last tube out, but I walked entirely by myself! Standing straight up and down, I made my way down the hall with a walker as my only support, listening to the soft beeps and whirrs of the other patients' machines.

At this point, I was finally healthy enough that I could and should have been transferred from the ICU to a different part of the hospital. "We'd like Kermit to stay until he leaves for Palo Alto," many nurses and doctors told Dr. O.

Agreeing, he nodded and said I could stay in the ICU as long as they didn't need my bed for another patient. Nobody did, so I was able to stay my last few days in the ICU, strengthening my grip on second place. Not that I'm competitive.

The day before we left, Kate walked in sporting an especially cheery mood. "Good morning, sunshine," she called to me. I half looked at her, giving no gesture or attempt at speaking in response. Kate continued trying to talk to me that morning without getting anything in return. Until she left for lunch, I either ignored her or slept. Ouch! Can you imagine?

Deeply hurt by my dismissive behavior, Kate felt partially sad and partially selfish for expecting more from someone in the ICU. Still, she found herself wondering, *Does Lang even still love me?* We were, after all, in uncharted territory. I was still healing and rebecoming myself. In a very real and accelerated way, I was in the early stages of repeating, in part, the stages of growth and development I'd already traveled as a kid, teenager, and young adult. Leaving the ICU was going to begin a new chapter in my life adventure, so she didn't know what to expect or whom the new Lang would choose.

On her return to the hospital, Kate lingered in the car for a long moment and prayed for God to give her a sign that I still loved her. Pausing at the threshold of my door, she closed her eyes and took a deep breath before turning the corner to walk into my room. There I sat, waiting for her with open arms. As a soft gasp escaped her lips, Kate dropped her purse and crossed the room to be wrapped in the tight embrace of my arms. When we finally broke apart, I noticed and pointed at her tears with concern. "They're tears of joy," she sighed happily.

Before the sun rose on January 7, 2009, Kate and I walked the ICU hall for the last time as visitor and patient. Smiling broadly, I gave a thumbs-up and waves to the nurses and doctors as we departed to their chorus of "Goodbye" and "Please come visit us."

After loading me into the ambulance, Kate got into my car, and off we drove to Palo Alto, California, for several months of inpatient rehabilitation. With the kind words and care of family, friends, and the hospital staff filling our hearts, we began a new journey. The future was unknown, but we could rest assured it'd be done with caring friends and family forming a ragtag band of love.

Words have power. They create worlds of wonder or domains of despair. They can call forth heaven or rain down hell.

I think there's a reason why the Jewish, Christian, and Islamic creation poem says God spoke things into existence. God did on a cosmic level what we all do every day. We fashion realities for both others and ourselves via what we say or don't say.

Small, mindful words or acts of kindness can make or break a person's day. And by that, I'm not just writing about what we share with others;, the same is also true of our inner critic or supporter. Aren't we often harder on ourselves than we would be on others or anyone else is on us? Sometimes incredibly so! We frequently beat ourselves up for mistakes and missteps more than others ever would, do we not?

Speaker, scholar, and *New York Times* best-selling author Brené Brown says all too often, the first thoughts in our heads in the morning are something along the lines of, "I'm not enough, I have too much to do, and there's no way I'll get it all done." This is why

I think it's essential for us to foster positivity, both toward others and ourselves.

Family, friends, coworkers, and medical staff surrounded me with encouragement, positivity, affirmations, and hope. Their words, gifts, letters, cards, and actions were life rafts in a storm I believe would have otherwise drowned me.

Kate frequently telling me how proud she was of me and regularly massaging my aching body, Leia calling me sunshine and reminding me how much she loved me, the encouraging Bible verses my mom lovingly posted around my room, the Sonics jerseys bought and worn by Josh and Karl, the meals made for my visiting family and friends, and more saved my life. These weren't forced or burdensome because not only does what's deepest within us desire to do good, but everyday kindness isn't hard; it's simple and makes a big difference.

I totally get life is hard at times; sometimes it's really hard. And even in those times, there is beauty to notice and point out. Hugs, high-fives, and fist bumps always bring more cheer to everyone involved. Truthful compliments to both yourself and others are totally doable. I'd go so far as to say people and life are always worth celebrating. After all, what could be truer when the most essential reality for us all is love?

We are each loved infinitely by the Source of all reality. Truthfully, nothing we could do or not do could make this love less or more. We're beloved children of the Divine Parent, period, full stop. This Creator declares each of us worthy and worth celebrating and invites us to a party and dance of love. Just as God has always done, eternally pouring God's self out for the thriving and flourishing of others, we are invited to join a divine dance party, one in which we give and receive life-giving and joy-bringing love forevermore.

The universe has a harmony. Existence has a bass note. Life has a dance. At the center of these is love and the longing for union, with one another and God. When we join hands and circle together as friends, family, and strangers, and as I did in this tale of love, we most fully and deeply hear and are moved by this rhythm.

If this book does anything, my fervent hope is this: May we hug more. May we smile a lot. May we compliment whenever possible. May we encourage and affirm regularly. May we frequently touch with love. May we celebrate constantly. May our words and actions bring heaven to earth, now. May we dance through life together to the rhythm of divine love. And may we sweetly fall into the arms of God's love together.

Epilogue

So, what do you think? With God on our side like this, how can we lose? If God didn't hesitate to put everything on the line for us, embracing our condition and exposing himself to the worst by sending his own Son, is there anything else he wouldn't gladly and freely do for us? And who would dare tangle with God by messing with one of God's chosen? Who would dare even to point a finger? The One who died for us—who was raised to life for us!—is in the presence of God at this very moment sticking up for us. Do you think anyone is going to be able to drive a wedge between us and Christ's love for us? There is no way! Not trouble, not hard times, not hatred, not hunger, not homelessness, not bullying threats, not backstabbing, not even the worst sins listed in Scripture:

"They kill us in cold blood because they hate you. We're sitting ducks; they pick us off one by one."

None of this fazes us because Jesus loves us. I'm absolutely convinced that nothing—nothing living or dead, angelic or demonic, today or tomorrow, high or low, thinkable or unthinkable—absolutely nothing can get between us and God's love because of the way that Jesus our Master has embraced us. (Romans 8:31–39 The Message)

My eyes blinked open. As the world came into a fuzzy focus, I gradually realized I was in an ambulance speeding along a highway in the middle of the desert. This image, my first memory since three days before the accident, is vivid and foggy, distinct and otherworldly. Disoriented, I had little grasp on what was going on or where I was headed, but this didn't trouble me as I rested peacefully in this truth: An incredible community of family and friends loves me deeply and well, mirrors of the Divine's affections that shine brighter than the sun.

With a shiver, I realized I was cold, so I called for Kate. "I need Kate," I told the EMT.

"We'll stop as soon as we can," he let me know.

At the next rest stop, they pulled over and let Kate know I was asking for her. As she ducked into the ambulance, she asked, "What do you need, Lang?"

"I'm cold," I replied.

Laughing in delight and glad I was actually able to speak at that moment, Kate told me, "Okay, we'll get another blanket on you. You can ask the EMT for things like that, you know."

As I smiled and nodded, they bundled me up, making me nice and cozy for the rest of the journey. Off into the unknown the ambulance ventured. None of us had any idea what the future had in store.

No one imagined I'd have to relearn how to properly walk or to emote verbally and facially. People wouldn't have guessed Kate and I would be married in just over three months. It didn't even cross my mind that the air force would retire me and I'd learn I couldn't drive again later that year. Neither would I ever have thought Kate and I would be divorced in just under five years.

Many pleasures and sorrows awaited me. Numerous highs and lows were still to come. Yet through them all, joy continually abounds. Divine love is always and forever the ground beneath our feet and our guide in both darkness and light.

Pictures

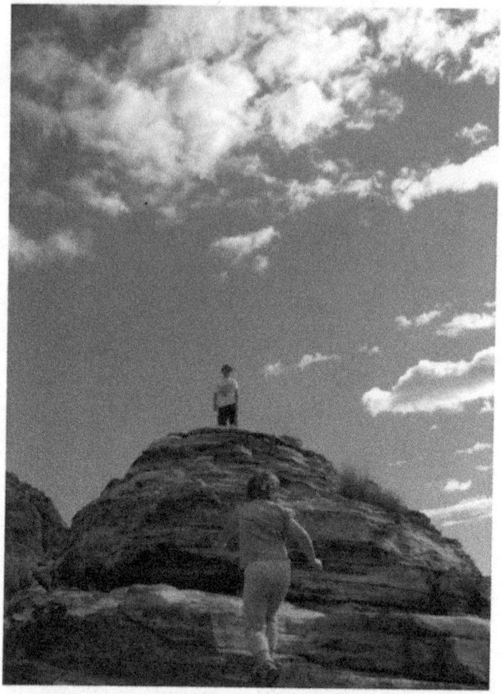

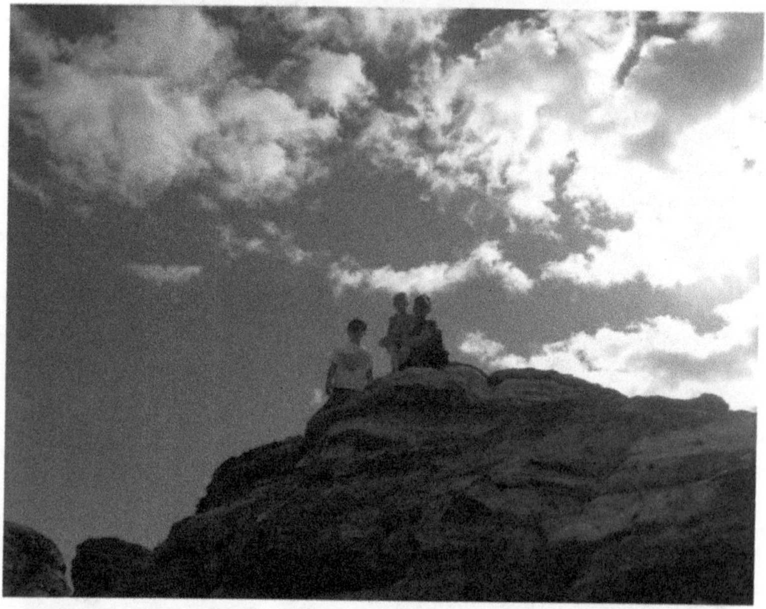

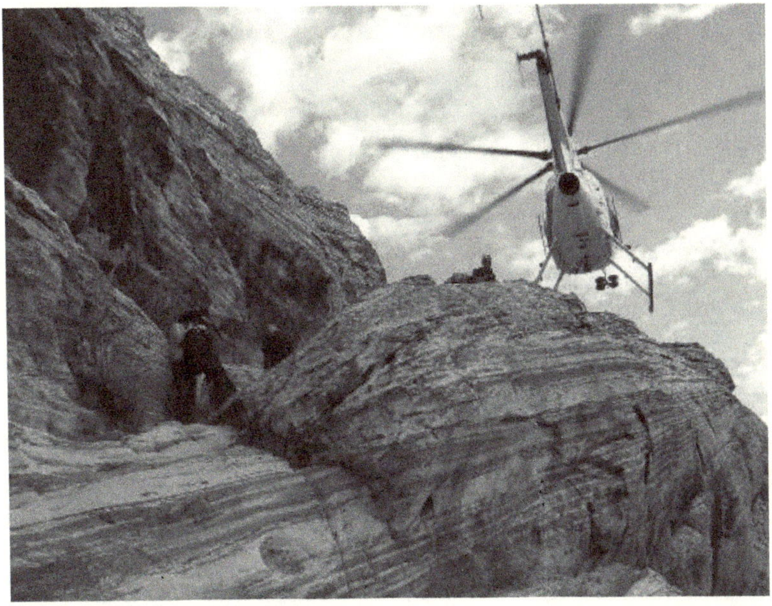

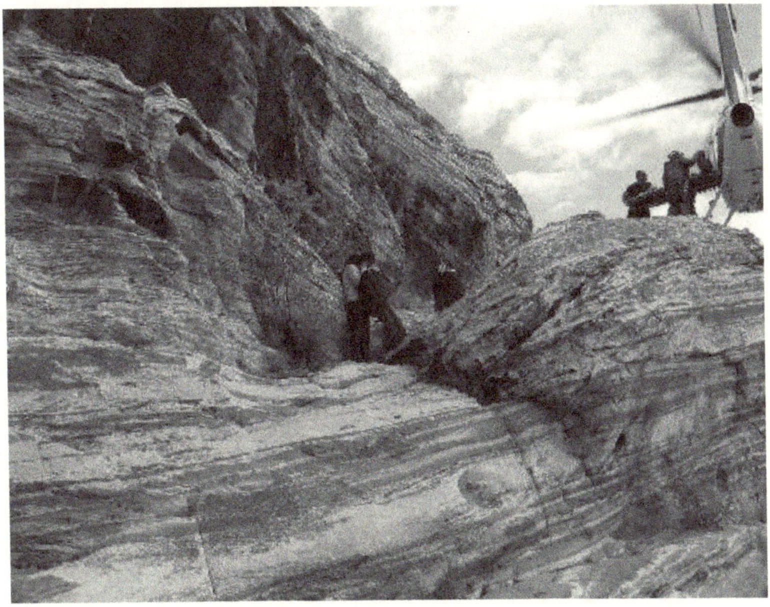

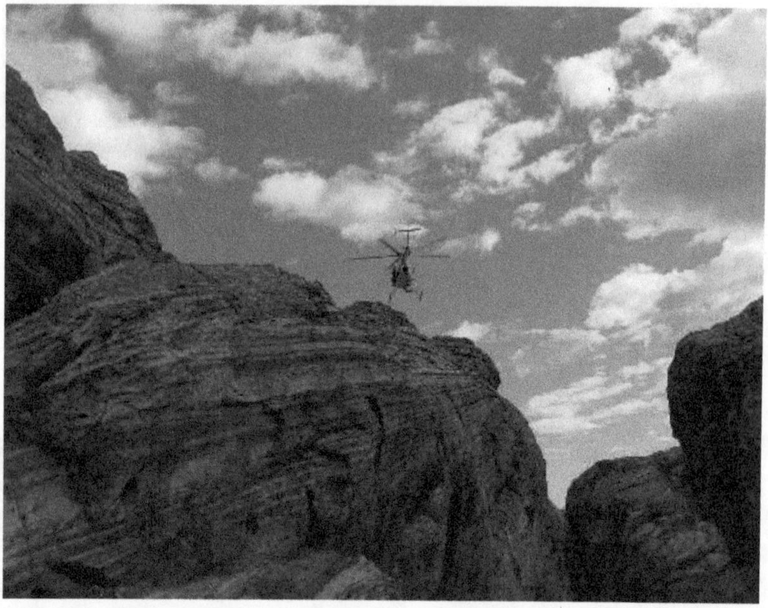

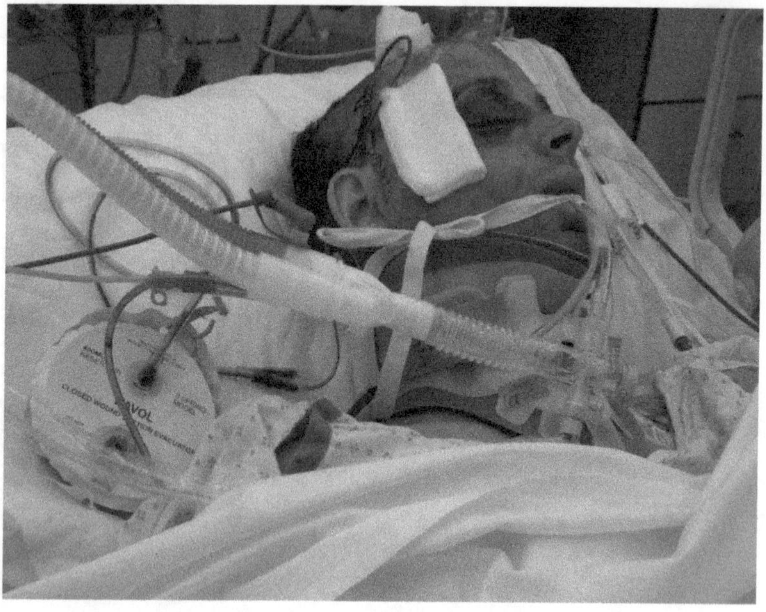

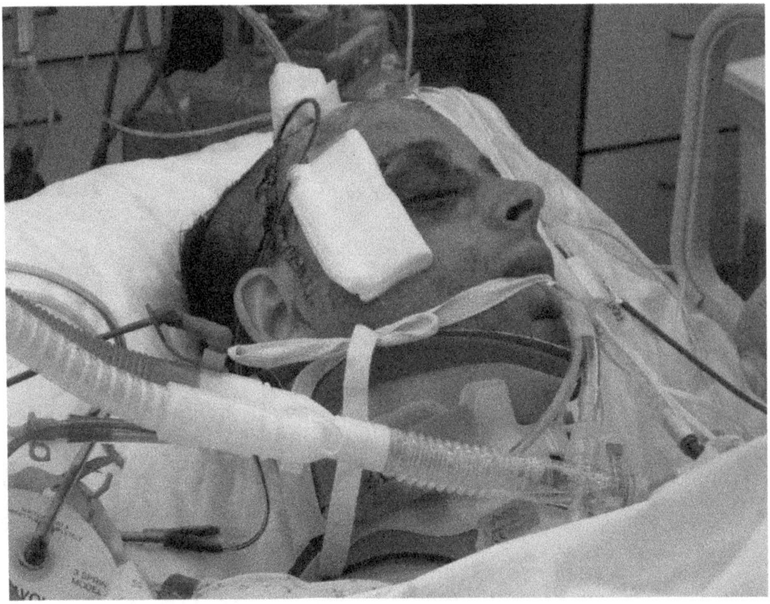

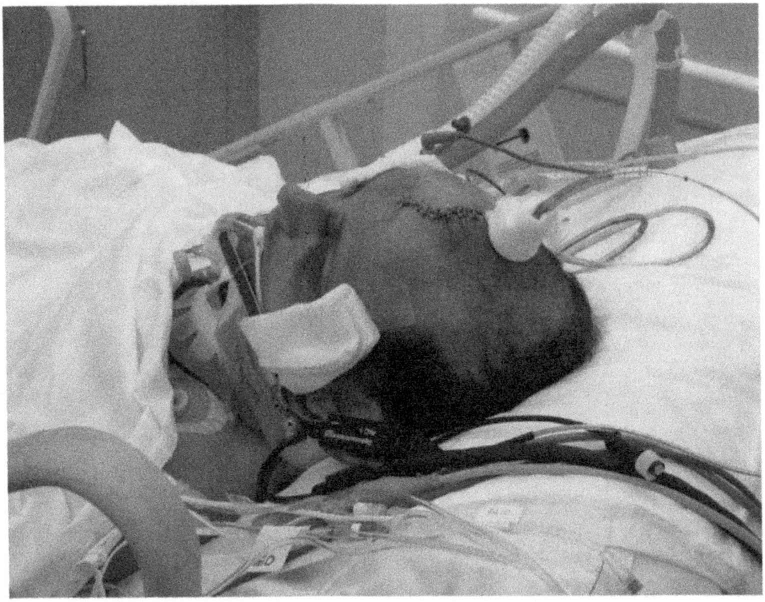

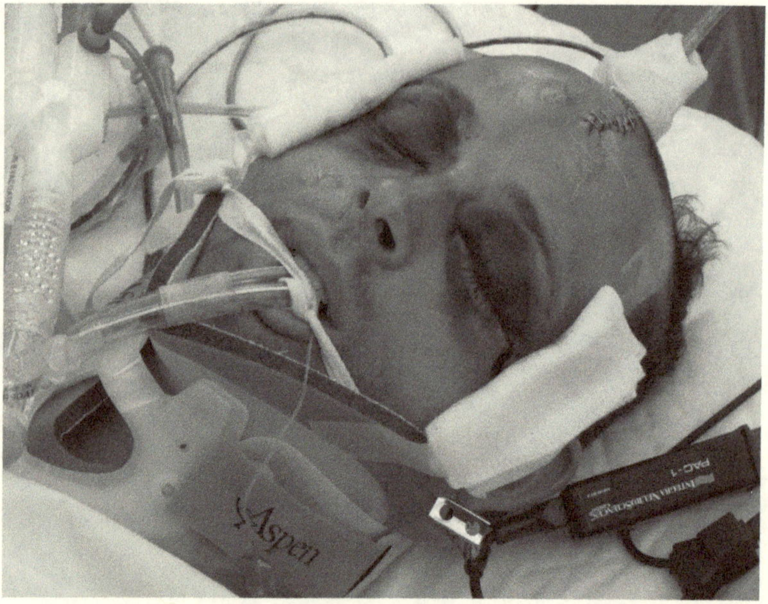
Aspen
PAC-1

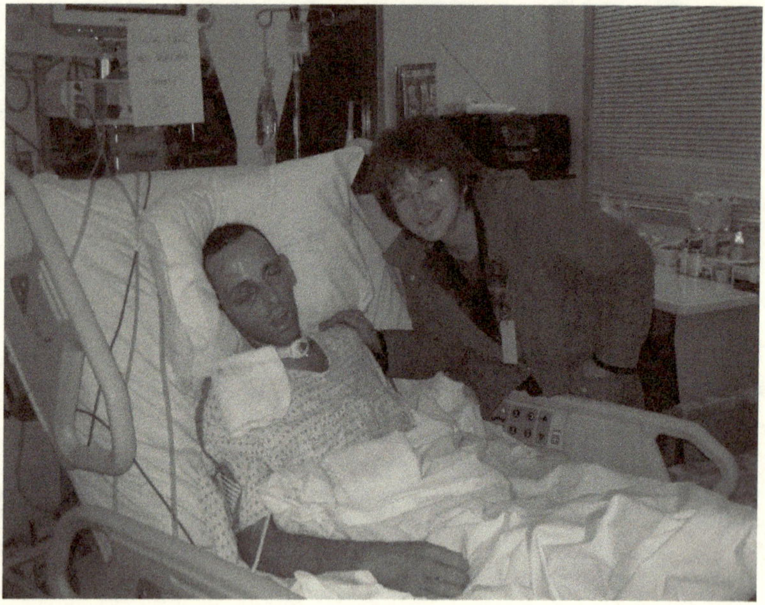

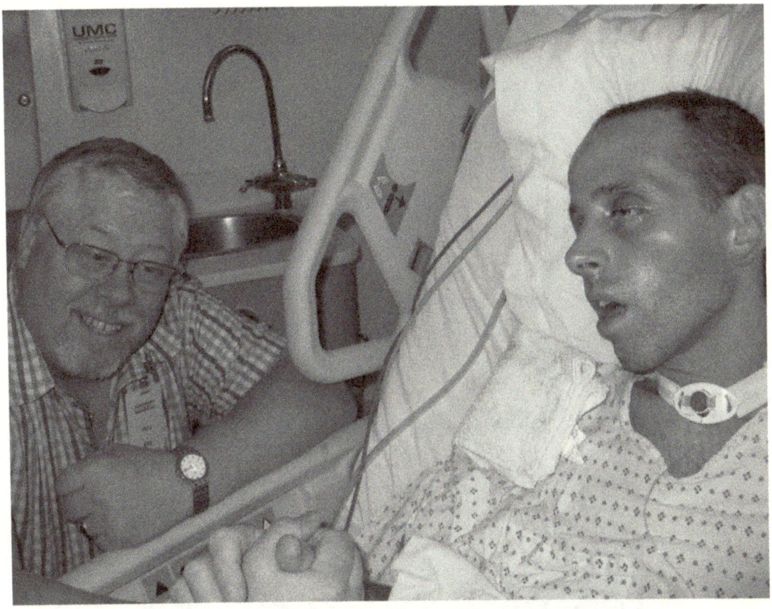
UMC

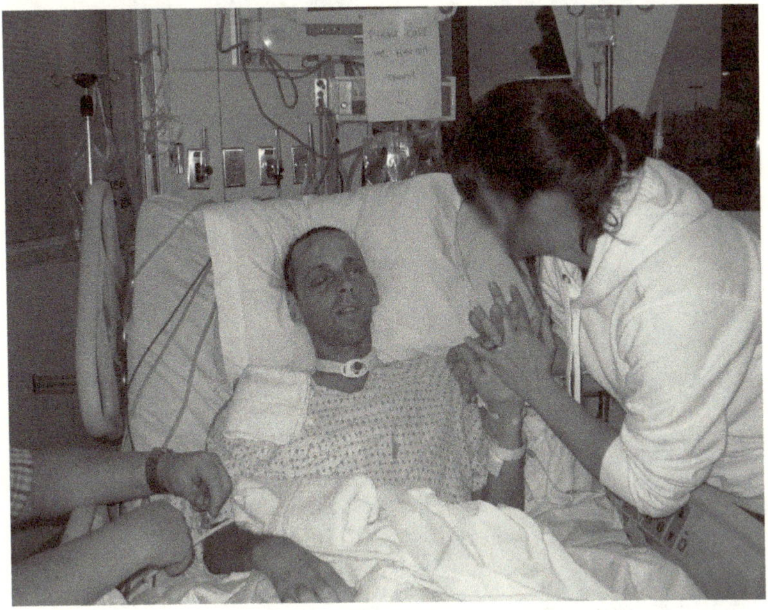

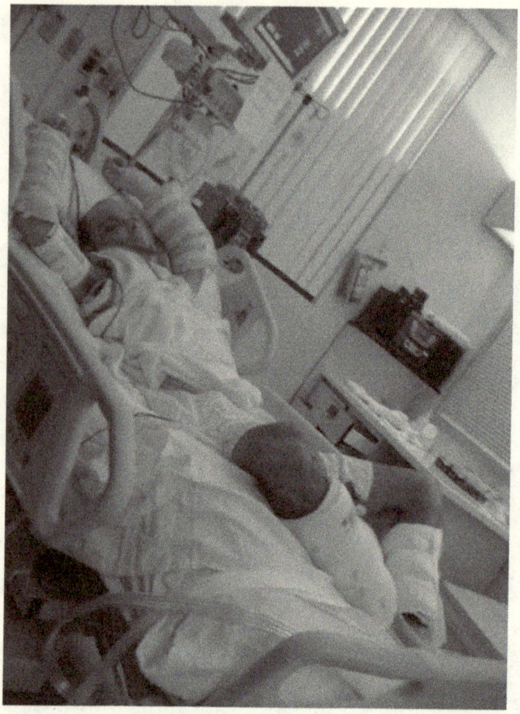

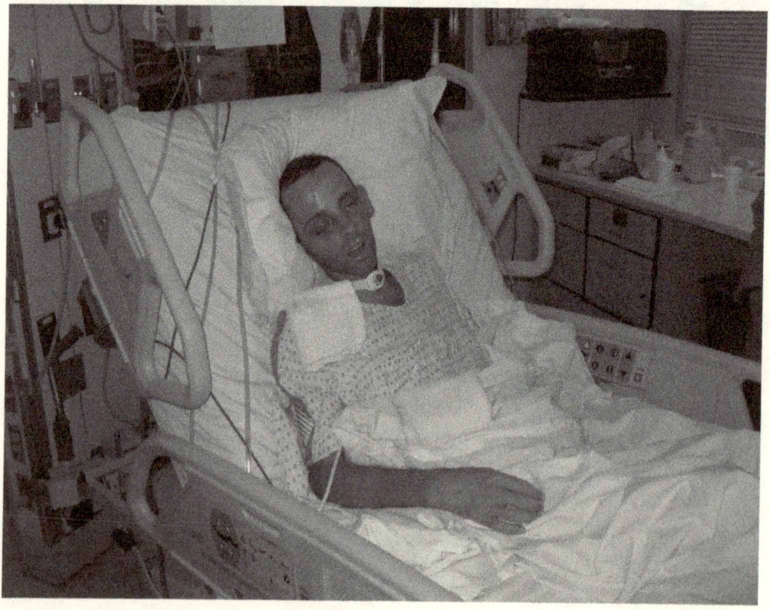

141

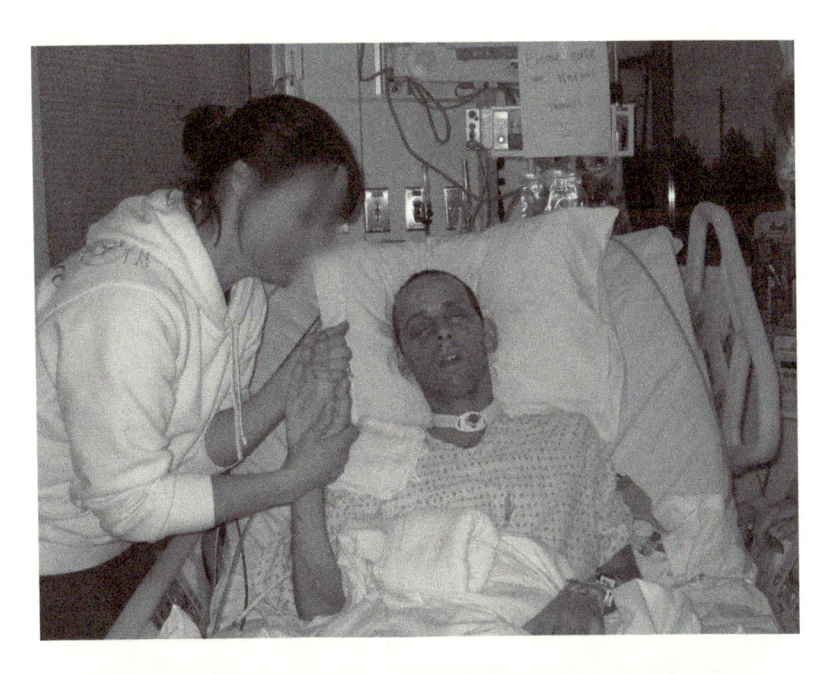

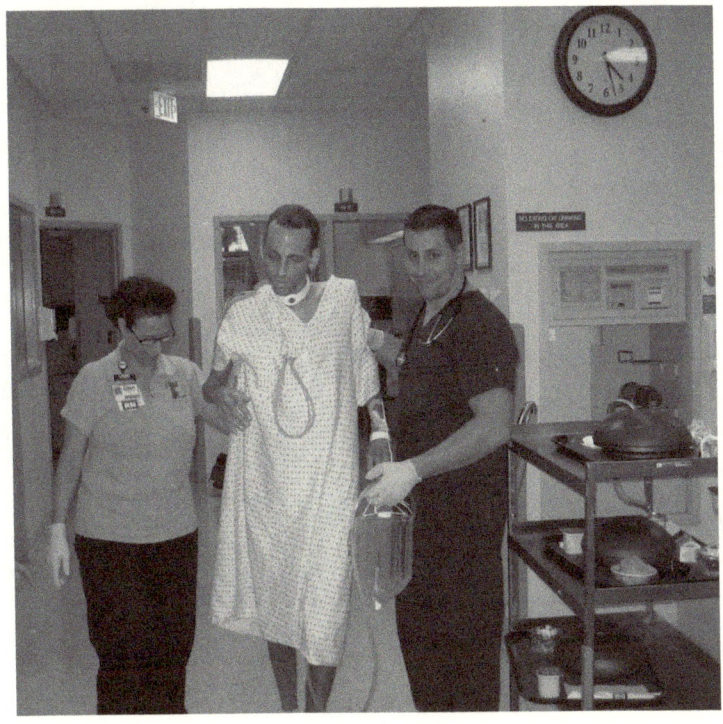

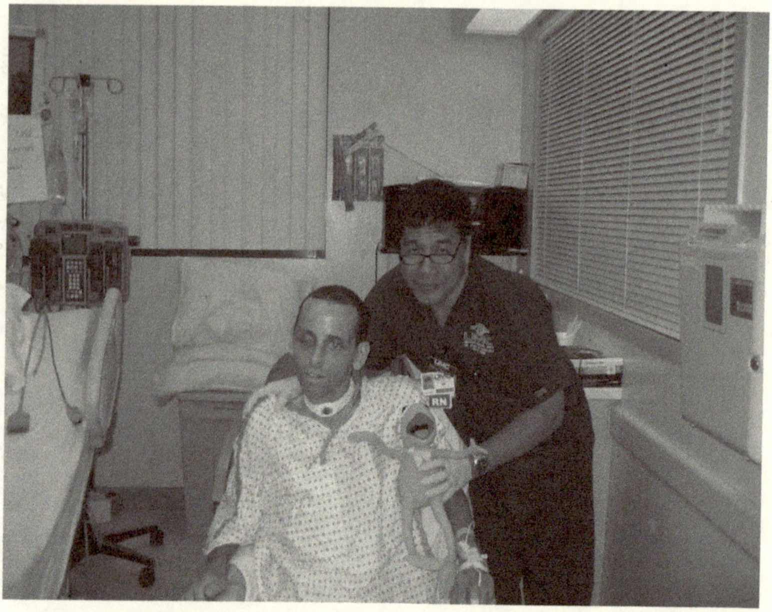
RN

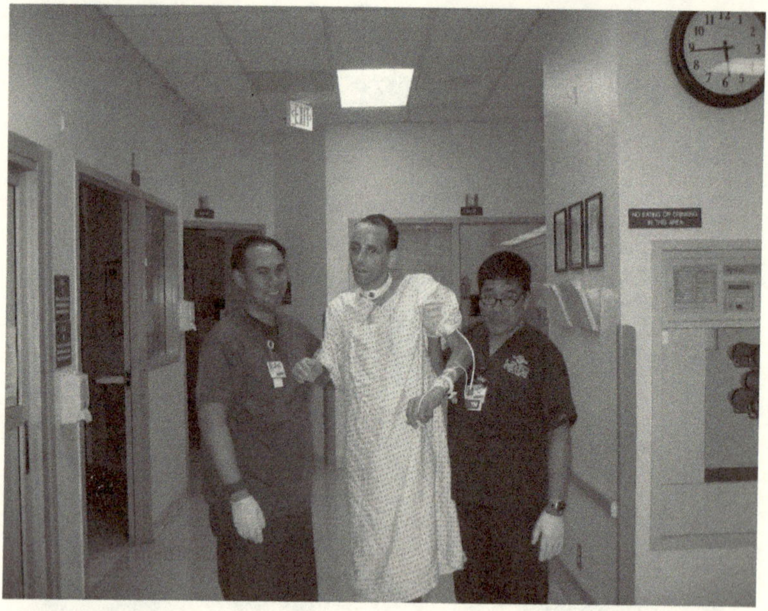
EXIT

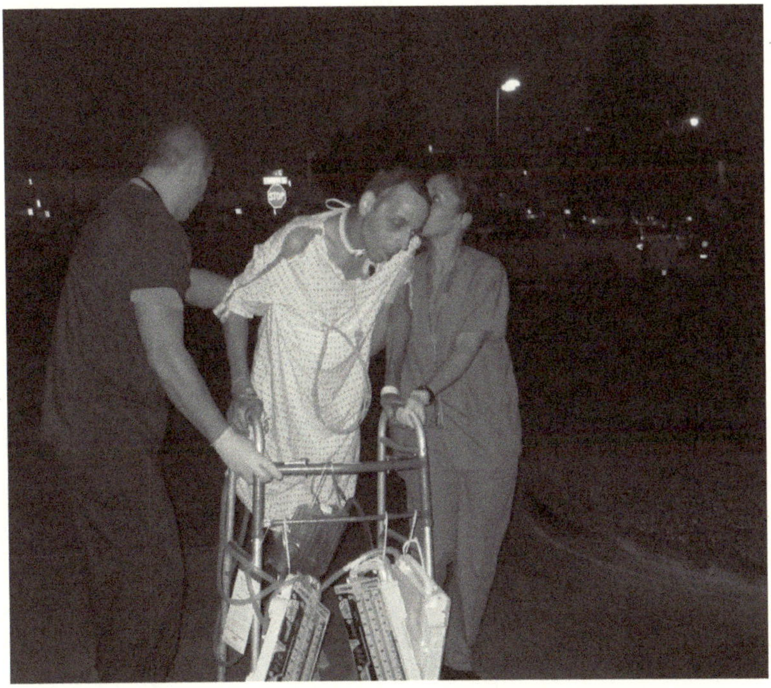
STOP